# Hibiscus

*Jacqueline Walker*

*Photographs by Gil Hanly*

**FIREFLY BOOKS**

The author and photographer wish to thank in particular Chris Noble, President of the Australian Hibiscus Society, and his wife Patricia Noble, of Hibiscus World, Caboolture, Queensland and François Paré of Gleuriste & Centre Jardin Scardera Ltée, Canada. They are also grateful to Rob Bayly, Joy Browne, Jack Clark, Gordon Currie, Bruce Haggo, Fane Kearney, Arno King, Jane Rumble, Dene Thomas, Bill Wilkie, Ron van Zuilen; and to all the gardeners who allowed their hibiscus to be photographed.

Photographs pages 79 and 80: Dr John Feltwell, Garden & Wildlife Matters Photo Library; photograph page 83: Charles Black.

Page 1: The glow of red hibiscus and the suggestion of the blue sea make a stunning combination. Page 2: 'Annie Wood' Page 3: 'Eden Rose'

## A FIREFLY BOOK

Published by Firefly Books Ltd. 2001

First Printing

Library of Congress Cataloging in Publication Data is available.

**Canadian Cataloguing in Publication Data**

Walker, Jacqueline
    Hibiscus

Includes bibliographical references and index.
ISBN 1-55209-563-0 (bound)  ISBN 1-55209-533-9 (pbk.)

Hibiscus. I. Title

SB413.H6W34 2001          635.9′33685          C00-931519-5

Published in the United States in 2001 by
Firefly Books (U.S.) Inc.
P.O. Box 1338, Ellicott Station
Buffalo, New York
14205

Published in Canada in 2001 by
Firefly Books Ltd.
3680 Victoria Park Avenue
Willowdale, Ontario
M2H 3K1

Visit our website at www.fireflybooks.com

Cover design by Shelley Watson
Book design by Errol McLeary
Typesetting by Jazz Graphics
Printed in Hong Kong by Colorcraft Ltd

# Contents

# Introduction

Hibiscus are paint-box plants. With colors so bold and petals so large, they're among the most flamboyant flowers in the world and easily recognized by the prominent staminal tube, typical of Malvaceae, the botanical family to which hibiscus belong. So dominant is this trait in all hibiscus, that in the species *Hibiscus schizopetalus*, the length of the elongated tube exceeds the diameter of the petals. Botanically, the structure is described as a merger of stamens and filaments fused together into a tube which arises from the base of the petals and surrounds the filiform style.

While all plant families have certain distinguishing features by which they are classified, kinship within each family is not always apparent. For example, Euphorbiaceae, a huge group that includes wafting garden perennials, tall trees and solitary desert cacti, can challenge the most astute botanist with its wide diversity. Malvaceae members are easier to identify. In addition to the central tube that is present in many, though not all, the flower formation of petals (usually five) is frequently arranged in an overlapping twist which is most conspicuous in the bud. Hibiscus flowers with this petal formation are referred to as "windmill type". There are other Malvaceae characteristics that the observer soon recognizes, including the bark and the calyxes containing the seedpods.

With more than 42 genera and more than 1000 species among its members, the Malvaceae family includes many plants of economic value, such as species that yield oil, paper and fiber, and others with medicinal properties. However, the two most cultivated are *Hibiscus*, grown today mostly ornamentally, and *Gossypium*, one of the world's most important crops, and one that has profoundly influenced political and economic history.

*Gossypium* produces cotton. There are several varieties, including G. *barbadense*, G. *herbaceum*, G. *tomentosum*, G. *hirsutum*, and G. *arboreum*, which is the cotton tree native to India. If you've ever wondered exactly which part of the plant yields the fluffy white stuff that's spun into thread enough to clothe nations, it's the filaments. After the flower (yellow with purple streaks and splodge at the base) withers, the leathery seedcase is left behind, and inside this, wrapped around the black seeds, is a mass of white fibers.

Writing in ancient Greece in the 5th century BC, Herodotus reported that in India "certain wild trees bear wool instead of fruit that in beauty and quality exceeds that of the sheep; and the Indians make their clothing from these trees." *Gossypium* is something of a wonder plant because the seeds yield edible oil and butter substitutes, while seed residue is used for stock feed, oilcloth, putty, fertilizer, soap and nitroglycerine.

Many Malvaceae species are edible, including hibiscus. Yes, those large, often plate-sized petals are not only luscious to look at, they're also – if not exactly luscious to eat – quite edible and quite nutritious. And though they may not be epicurean in flavor, their bright colors can enliven a salad. More flavorsome and extensively grown as a food crop is *Hibiscus esculentus* (syn *Abelmoschus esculentus*), the vegetable known as "okra".

Opposite: The pendulous flower of the species *Hibiscus schizopetalus* (from *schizo* meaning "split" to describe the deeply divided petals) has an exceptionally long staminal tube in proportion to the petals.

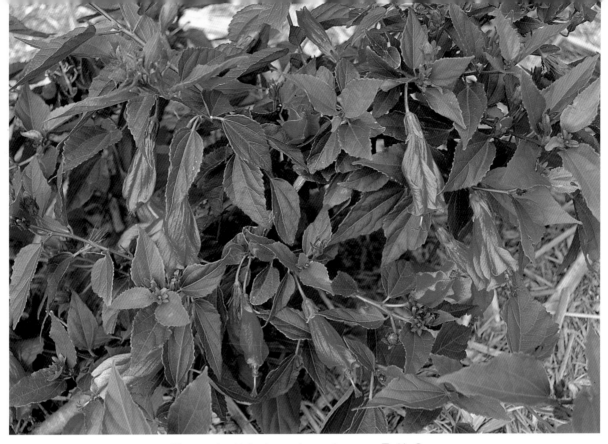

The species *Malvaviscus arboreus*, known as Turk's Cap, has flowers that never fully open.

Other Malvaceae species in garden culture include *Abutilon*, the Chinese lantern or flowering maple, elegant in both leaf and flower and well-adapted to mild and temperate gardens; *Alcea rosea* (syn *Althaea rosea*), the popular hollyhock; *Malva parviflora*; *Malvastrum coromandelinum*, the false mallow; *Sida fallax*, once popularly used in Hawaiian leis; *Pavonia hastata*, the pastel flowering shrub; *Lavatera*, favorite of gardeners everywhere; and the well-known *Malvaviscus arboreus* or Turk's Cap. But hibiscus are the showpiece of the Malvaceae, and the tropical hybrids bred from hibiscus species indigenous to many countries have produced some of the most dazzling of all cultivated flowers. With more and more breeding has come more and more variety. Hybrid after hybrid has been released into the gardening marketplace so that there is now an almost limitless choice in shrub shape, height, spread, habit and foliage, as well as, of course, the main reason for growing these plants – the sumptuous blooms.

It is hybrids rather than species that are the subject of these chapters. The following advice on cultivation, pruning and maintenance, selection and landscape design applies generally to these modern hybrids. In Chapter 4, Hibiscus in Cool Climates, the cultivation of hardier species and their hybrids, together with selected close cousins of hibiscus, is considered separately.

While tropical hybrids hold the limelight, species have not been banished from cultivation. Many still grow and proliferate in the wild, and others continue to be grown in gardens around the world. Some important hot-climate species include: *H. brackenridgei* (Pua Aloalo in Hawaiian), a yellow-flowering species endemic to Hawaii, and the state's flower; *H. elatus*, which yields fiber from the inner bark and is still used today for wrapping cigars; *H. calyphyllus* from tropical Africa; *H. cameronii* from Madagascar, significant for its use in the breeding of many hybrids; *H. clayii*, another Hawaiian plant; *H. coccineus*, a brilliant red and large-flowered

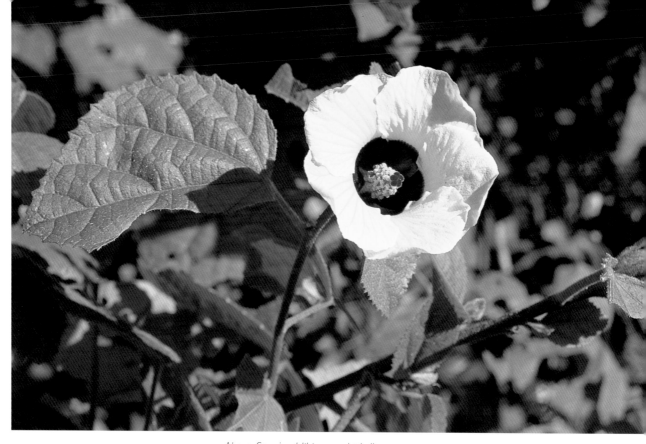

*Above:* Species *Hibiscus calyphyllus*
Below left: Species *Hibiscus coccineus* a species indigenous to southeast U.S.A.
Below right: Species *Hibiscus clayii*

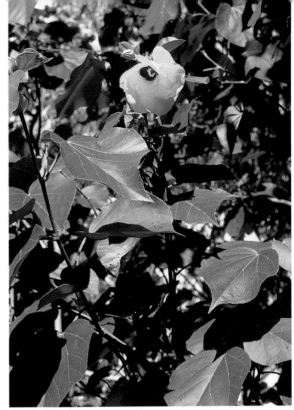

Above left: *Hibiscus sabdariffa*: the calyxes of this species are made into jelly. Above right: *Hibiscus tiliaceus*, "the cotton tree", is common to coastal regions throughout the tropical and sub-tropical Pacific, where it grows into a large tree. All parts of the tree have been used in traditional cultures.

herbaceous hibiscus native to southeast U.S.A. and one of the most popularly grown species; *H. youngianus*, native to the marshlands of Hawaii; *H. liliiflors*, from the Seychelles; *H. pedunculatus* from Africa; *H. sabdariffa*, a biennial often grown as an annual for its fruits, the enlarged calyxes, which make "rosella jam", once commercially produced from crops in Queensland; *H. schizopetalus*, the species with the split petals and extra-long staminal tube; *H. splendens*, a small tree native to Australia, with exceptionally lovely flowers, widely-grown and admired; and *H. tiliaceus*, a large tree common to all tropical and sub-tropical regions of the world and once the source of Pacific islands' tapa cloth.

In all, the hibiscus genus comprises about 250 species – possibly more. Many are herbaceous and low ground plants, some grow into shrubs of shoulder height, and others into large trees. They are found mostly in climates that are tropical and sub-tropical rather than temperate. However, the hybrid progeny of these species have been bred for more cold tolerance. As a result, today's hybrids grow well outdoors in the sub-tropics and moderately well in temperate climates, while not really flourishing in the true tropics. Sub-tropical climates are distinguished from the tropics by their discernible – though slight – winter chill. Although mild, such winters are sufficient to induce a rest period, followed by spring-triggered new growth. These climates suit hibiscus well. It's here, where spring temperatures rise only a notch or two, that they take time to reach their peak, but when they do they excel, their flowers continuing long into the fall.

Beyond the tropics and sub-tropics, potted hibiscus fill a different role. Along with bringing out the deck chairs from winter storage, containered plants are brought out from indoors, to revive in spring sunshine after their hibernation. The method is convenient and instant – and guaranteed to lift the spirits! Pots can be positioned to help with flowering, while their portable decorative value is well-suited to restricted spaces. With such bold flowers and bright colors, is it any wonder hibiscus can stop you in your tracks?

# Hardiness Zone Map

This map has been prepared to agree with a system of plant hardiness zones that have been accepted as the international standard and range from 1 to 11. It shows the minimum winter temperatures that can be expected on average in different regions.

In this book, where a zone number has been given, the number indicates the coldest areas in which the particular plant is likely to survive through an average winter.

Note that these are not necessarily the areas in which it will grow best. Because the zone number refers to the minimum temperatures, a plant given Zone 7, for example, will obviously grow perfectly well in Zone 8, but not in Zone 6. Plants grown in a zone considerably higher than the zone with the minimum winter temperature in which they will survive might grow well, but they are likely to behave differently. Note also that some readers may find the numbers a little conservative; we felt it best to err on the side of caution.

| °F | Zone | °C |
|---|---|---|
| below -50 | 1 | below -45 |
| -50 to -40 | 2 | -45 to -40 |
| -40 to -30 | 3 | -40 to -34 |
| -30 to -20 | 4 | -34 to -29 |
| -20 to -10 | 5 | -29 to -23 |
| -10 to 0 | 6 | -23 to -16 |
| 0 to 10 | 7 | -16 to -12 |
| 10 to 20 | 8 | -12 to -7 |
| 20 to 30 | 9 | -7 to -1 |
| 30 to 40 | 10 | -1 to 4 |
| above 40 | 11 | above 4 |

Hardiness zones are based on
the average annual minimum
temperature for each zone.

CHAPTER 1

# *History*

If the name "hibiscus" brings to mind palm-fringed islands, coral atolls and shaded verandas, it's not surprising, for hibiscus are coastal plants and have grown for centuries around the rim of the Indian and Pacific oceans. Colonialism in the 18th and 19th centuries helped give the flower its romantic image, an image exploited today by tourist advertising that seeks to sell holidays to oceanic destinations, to lure travelers to places of leisurely living. The name alone sells. Resorts, real-estate companies, retirement villages and restaurants use it: there's "Hibiscus Hotel", "Hibiscus Health Spa" … even a clothing label. (And a check on the Internet shows that the word "hibiscus" appears in 997,940 entries.)

The name may be well-known but its origins are not. Hibiscus is understood to derive from the Greek word *hibiskos*, given by the Greek physician Dioscorides in the 1st century to the marshmallow plant, a close relative of the hibiscus.

*Hibiscus rosa-sinensis*, an old species that was grown as an ornamental flower in China, is believed to have been cultivated there for hundreds, if not thousands, of years – so long in fact that there is no record of it being found in the wild. Although it appears to have been in cultivation throughout much of the Asian continent, early reports of *H. rosa-sinensis* flowering around temples in China imply a Chinese origin, hence the name "sinensis".

When this species was introduced further afield it adapted especially well in those places where other hibiscus species already grew. Everywhere the potent red-petalled flower of *H. rosa-sinensis* was seen, it

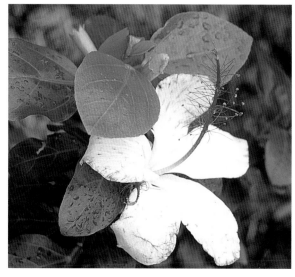

Above: *Hibiscus arnottianus* a species from Hawaii.
Opposite: *Hibiscus rosa-sinensis*, the species used extensively in hybridizing.

gained a following. It was admired in the Chelsea Physic Garden in London, in Europe, India, Africa and North America, to the point that it became the celebrated flower of the tropics. The existence of other species growing in these countries enabled horticulturists to take the next step and cross *H. rosa-sinensis* with some of these. Though many of these species' flowers were less flamboyant, when genetically blended with the bold red newcomer, the results were spectacular. Thus encouraged, they tried further crossing – and behold, today's handsome tropical hybrids were born.

Enthusiasm in Hawaii claimed a lot of attention. Using three indigenous species, including the pearl-white *H. arnottianus*, which is scented, together with

more than 33 others imported from other countries
– notably the East African species *H. schizopetalus*,
as well as *H. cameronii* – Hawaiian hybridists crossed
and recrossed them in an extensive program that
produced a total of more than 5000 horticultural
varieties. ("Horticultural" here means that the
genetic parentage was recorded and the offspring
identified, but not that there were 5000 varieties
worthy of further propagation and promotion. On
the contrary: in hybridizing trials only about one in
every 100 or 200 will produce desirable properties of
good form, foliage, flower and all-around
performance.)

New tropical hybrids were created from the most
successful of these – large and luscious in bloom,
riveting in color, and impressive in range. By now
the hybrids had eclipsed the species, and so eagerly
did Hawaiians embrace them that not only was the
first hibiscus society formed there in 1911, but in
1923 a law was passed making the flower the symbol
of the territory of Hawaii. Today the flower is still
enshrined in law – after Hawaii joined the U.S.A. its
emblem became the state flower – and it continues
to delight residents as much as visitors.

Bountiful and bold, sirens of islands, hibiscus
became the symbol of many Polynesian and
Micronesian cultures, their flowers bedecking
doorways and feasting tables as tokens of welcome,
while in Indian Ocean cultures the sacred hibiscus
decorated temples and religious offerings.

By the mid-20th century intensive hybridizing
work was being done in Florida, and the focus of
attention shifted from Hawaii to southeastern
U.S.A. Later still, Australian horticulturists began
trialing new cultivars with unprecedented success.
By the 1980s there were over 4000 recognized
tropical hybrids in cultivation. Today there are more
than 10,000 hybrids worldwide.

Throughout all of this breeding, *H. rosa-sinensis*
remained the most important genetic parent, but it
was not the only species used. Confusingly, it is now
difficult to establish with accuracy which tropical

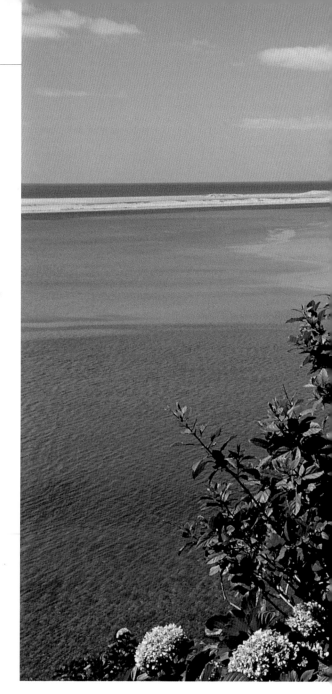

hybrids are the progeny of *H. rosa-sinensis* and which
are not. Indeed, the need for clarification of the
general use of the term "*rosa-sinensis* hybrids" is
overdue. There are Fijian hybrids and Hawaiian
hybrids that are not derived from *H. rosa-sinensis*
(and some that did once, but so far back in their
ancestry that it's been bred out), together with many
hybrids of unrecorded parentage. The solution? To
call them all, simply, tropical hybrids.

The Royal Horticultural Society has formally adopted the recent proposal of the International Registrar to label them "*Hibiscus rosa-sinensis* and its sexually compatible species and its cultivars". This term covers all tropical hybrids, together with their species parents, whether or not *H. rosa-sinensis* played a part in their creation. At the same time it sets them apart from other species that have never been crossed with – i.e. have proved to be incom-patible with – *H. rosa-sinensis*, such as the deciduous and herbaceous plants that grow in cool climates and are described in Chapter 4.

Above: Hibiscus are always at home in coastal settings.

CHAPTER 2

# Outdoor Cultivation of Tropical Hibiscus

N ote on hardiness zones: Tropical hibiscus grow best in the mild hardiness Zones 11 and 12, and in parts of Zone 10 where there are niche microclimates. When given the special care suggested in Chapter 4, they may well thrive in the cooler parts of Zone 10. In areas cooler than these zones, container culture, as outlined in Chapter 9, is recommended. See the map on page 11 for further information on hardiness zones.

## Basic requirements for healthy growth

Hibiscus have four basic needs. These are sun and warmth, sharp drainage, ample moisture and nutrients. A further requirement, pruning, is covered in Chapter 6.

### Sun and warmth

Hibiscus should be planted in the warmest part of the garden where they receive day-long sun. The cooler the climate the more important it is to give them sheltered warmth in bright sunlight. Closer to the tropics these conditions aren't as crucial, and in fact growers in these lower latitudes have found that shrubs planted in part-shade, such as under the serrated umbrella of palm fronds, grow as well as or better than those in full sun.

Warmth means an absence of cold drafts, and again this is more of a challenge in cool climates where walls or fine-meshed trellises can give protection, and where raised beds with higher

Opposite: The health of these hybrids is evident in the dense, glossy foliage and the many buds ensuring flowering continuity.

edging can cosset roots, especially when mulched, while at the same time ensuring drainage. Warmth also means an absence of very low temperatures. A short cold-snap in winter as low as 37°F (3°C) is about the limit for these plants.

If finding a suitably sunny site is so difficult that there appears to be nowhere to plant your yearned-for hibiscus – well, go ahead and plant it in semi-shade. The foliage will be sparser and the flowers fewer, but it will certainly grow there, even if it doesn't thrive. (And don't give up. Garden conditions change. The neighbor's tall tree that overhangs your hibiscus may yet be cut back, or may die, or …?) Another solution to the lack of a sunny site is container culture, which may allow a plant to be moved around as the seasons dictate.

### Drainage

Good drainage is vital. If there is the remotest chance that the roots of your hibiscus might become waterlogged at times of prolonged rain, elevate the plant. Site it on higher ground, on the top of banks and slopes, or use raised beds. Or, if this is not possible, dig out the area and build a base of rocks and gravel before backfilling. Porous soils suit hibiscus. Fast-draining volcanic soil is good; sandy loam is ideal. Coastal sites which are almost pure sand may pose other challenges, such as how to provide and retain consistent moisture and nutrients, but drainage is not one of them.

The requirement is for aeration of the roots: hibiscus need a higher than average air-filled porosity. "Air-filled porosity" is a term used in the nursery industry to indicate the percentage, by volume, of air spaces in a container of potting mix that has been watered to saturation point and then allowed to drain off. A mix containing an abundance of coarse particles will have a high air-filled porosity. As an example, roses grow best where the air-filled porosity is about 10-12 percent. Epiphytic plants, which in nature grow in the forks of trees, need a growing medium of about 50-60 percent. While most bedding shrubs in cultivation prefer a lower percentage, the potting mix or soil best suited to hibiscus should have an air-filled porosity of about 25-30 percent.

Note that this drainage imperative applies to all hybrids and cultivated species, with the exception of *H. moscheutos* and *H. diversifolius*, which are described in Chapter 4. These two species flourish in swampy soils.

## Moisture

Hibiscus enjoy high humidity, but they'll grow happily in dry areas provided their roots have constant access to water, and provided their foliage is misted or regularly hosed. They need water most during the growing season. This means regular, thorough soaking. The faster the drainage, as in sandy beach gardens, the more watering will be needed. During the cold months of winter when the uptake of water is less, as it is with all garden plants, the need for watering will be less. In cooler climates with wet winters, watering will be unnecessary.

To test for moisture, examine the top few inches of surface soil. When it feels dry – really dry – your hibiscus needs water, and, as all experienced gardeners know, one infrequent but very thorough soaking is far better than lots of frequent but light sprinklings that may not penetrate.

Hibiscus's need for water goes hand-in-hand with the importance of mulching, which conserves moisture (see page 20), and with their requirement for regular feeding.

## Nutrients

Hibiscus grown in the ground do best when planted in well-prepared sites that have friable, loamy, good-quality soil with a pH reading of about 6 to 7, and plenty of organic matter that is routinely replenished. They really flourish if, during the warm months of active growth, they're given sustained nutrition. Potassium in particular should be in their diet as it promotes the best blooms, brightest color and most profuse flowering.

Many growers claim success with citrus fertilizer. Others testify to results with commercial rose and vegetable fertilizers, and if you have these on hand you can try them. Most nurseries use chemical nutrients in soluble form.

Chemical fertilizers have their advocates and garden-center salespeople are always happy to advise on the use of these products.

Certainly, slow-release granules are convenient for hibiscus in containers, but if you really care about the environment, if you're really attuned to the ground you walk on, the air you breathe, the water you use and the water you waste, if the clear distinction between organic and inorganic is instinctive, if you are conscious of the disposal of *everything* you consume, and if you eschew toxic pesticides and herbicides, then you will bypass these packets of pricey chemicals and go organic. Even the smallest garden has room for a pair of modest compost bins, and new models have been designed for tiny, tidy backyards. And when it comes to growing edible plants in compost, the results are incontestably superior – but this is to digress: if the organic path is one you've not ventured far along, there's plenty of information to be found.

Back to hibiscus. They thrive on compost. All organic matter, including well-decomposed manure, is beneficial because it supplies nutrients to the roots, promotes a healthy balance of organisms, and adds texture to the soil. The compost you give your hibiscus should be well aged. If you're in a position to prepare your planting site several months in

'Simmond's Red'

advance, you can use fresh manure; otherwise make sure it's well-rotted. Dried manure, such as packaged sheep pellets, can be used at any time. You can also dig in decomposing leaf mold or straw, or purchased peat moss. Mix it in thoroughly.

Like all plants, hibiscus need nitrogen, calcium, phosphorus, potassium, magnesium and sulfur as well as trace elements. Good-quality soil that is regularly enriched with organic matter should contain all of these – analyses of seaweed, for example, show it to contain every nutrient known to plants, and comfrey has similar properties – although occasionally there may be a need for supplementary additives. Dolomite is useful in providing magnesium and can modify a soil that is too acidic. Borax supplies the trace element boron; potash supplies potassium. If your soil is seriously deficient, the problem will show up not only in your

hibiscus but in other plants as well, in which event it would be wise to consult a soil expert.

Maintenance feeding means lightly digging in beyond the outer limits of the shallow roots, taking care not to disturb them, as well as applying compost on the surface. Liquid feeding can also be used. How often should you feed? During the growing season hibiscus have a vigorous uptake of nutrients and can be fed as often as every five or six weeks. In cooler climates (Zone 8 or less) feeding can be lighter.

Sub-tropical climates often experience forceful downpours of rain that can leach the soil of soluble nutrients, which is one reason for heavier feeding and mulching. Hand-watering, as distinct from nature's deluge, should always be done after feeding, and is essential if you use chemical fertilizers.

You can make your own liquid sprays for foliar feeding. A very diluted solution of liquid seaweed

In marginal climates hibiscus benefit from raised beds, and from the protection offered by walls and corners of buildings. (Pictured here, 'Madonna'.)

(i.e. after the seaweed itself has been removed) can be beneficial, but not every grower has access to the sea, and most home growers have to rely on their local garden retailers. There are now available a number of organic fish and marine solutions that you can buy in concentrated form and dilute for spraying. Organic gardening magazines often list similar preparations of good quality and lower prices in their classified advertisements.

Hibiscus fed little and often will be healthier than those fed heavily but infrequently.

## Mulching

The value of mulching cannot be overemphasized. Mulching preserves moisture and reduces the need to water by slowing down the rate of evaporation. At the same time the loose, coarse texture of mulch aids aeration. It can also add nutrients to the soil as it breaks down, and it inhibits the growth of weeds.

To some extent hibiscus are self-mulching in that they drop leaves and flowers almost year-round and these slowly decompose – another reason for never digging the soil at the base of the trunk. By all means dig a moat or shallow trench beyond the leaf drip-line and use this both for compost feeds and for placing mulch to spread over the center, but never dig down into the soil at the shrub's base. The area of the leaf drip-line is the area of the roots, i.e. the root area is defined by the diameter of the outermost foliage. It is within this circle that mulch should be applied – but don't pack it right up to the stem.

So, keeping clear of the trunk's base, apply your mulch as thickly as 6-8 in (15-20 cm), although it is best to apply it more thinly, say 2-4 in (5-10 cm) and top up regularly. The weather, too, can be an indicator of how thickly and how often to mulch: in droughts, apply more.

Now to mulch materials. Use any, or a mix of, the following: pine needles, leaf mold, straw (barley and pea straw are both excellent), hay, corn husks, nut husks, chopped or shredded prunings (not infected or infested, of course), rinsed seaweed, peat products, shredded newspaper (not colored or gloss), tree-fern fiber, coconut fiber, dried pine cones, bark (fresh pine bark should be avoided because it leaches too much resin, but small quantities can be mixed with other materials), spent mushroom compost, by-products of the sugar cane industry, or anything similar. Fresh lawn clippings should not be used, other than in small quantities mixed in with other materials. A very effective and stable mulch can be had from discarded doormats made of open-weave sisal (or coir or jute) – they're organic and make excellent aerating covers that decompose slowly.

# Hibiscus selection, siting, planting and staking

## Selection and siting

Today's tropical hybrids give the gardener far greater range in shape, size, habit and flower than was known a decade or so ago. Although pruning can enable you to keep a bush at whatever size you want, it makes more sense to select appropriately at the start.

Specialist growers and hibiscus society officials now recognize three sizes: tall (6-10 ft/2-3 m), medium (3-6 ft/1-2 m), and low (under 3 ft, or 1 m), in addition to the occasional very tall, or very low to almost prostrate. Note the use of the term, "low" rather than "miniature": unlike camellias, rhododendrons and other shrubs where "miniature" describes the overall size of the bush, in hibiscus culture the description refers to flower size, not shrub size.

There is also a three-fold classification of form: open, upright or bushy. Leaves should also be considered. All tropical hibiscus are evergreen, and leaf variation extends from the almost circular leaf to the very narrow, with many in between, while leaf margins can vary from smooth, or slightly serrated, to highly indented.

As for flower classification, this is almost a specialist subject in itself, so great is the variety that modern breeding has produced. The formal registration of hybrids and the need for uniform standards in show judging have called for some rules of conformity. Hibiscus societies now recognize four sizes of blooms: miniature (under 4 in, or 10 cm), medium (4-6 in/10-15 cm), large (6-8 in/15-20 cm), and extra large (8 in, or 20 cm, and over). (This last category may seem very desirable to many hibiscus lovers, but because such huge blooms are man-made rather than nature-made creations, they're often top-heavy. Beginner growers especially should regard them with caution.)

Besides these four flower sizes, and besides the three categories of single, double and semi-double, there are many forms and textures. Forms include cartwheel and cartwheel overlap (twisted formation of the base of the petals – wheel-like); windmill (narrower petals separated by gaps between each); fringed petals (outer edges are split and fringed); crested (both single and double forms may have this petaloidal or small petal-like growth on the style tip); cup-and-saucer (a central tuft of petaloids arises from the center and is distinctly separated from the outside petals); and recurved (the outer edges of the petals curve backwards). Petal textures include fluted (waves or soft ribs), ruffled, veined (contrasting color visible as thread-like veins) and picot or frilled edges.

From the grower's point of view, the main consideration – apart from, obviously, choosing the varieties that most appeal – is the space and location for the intended plant. Consider the ultimate size of each hibiscus you buy. You are the best judge of the best plants for the best places in your garden. And when you buy, make sure you select plants that show vitality: strong stems, good healthy foliage, and signs of plentiful new growth.

## Planting and transplanting

Always plant out in spring, at the start of the growing season. In mild climates (Zone 11 or above) it may be possible to plant from late-winter through to fall, but caution is best where weather is doubtful. The shock of a too-early planting in spring can be fatal in cool areas, as can a delayed fall attempt when winter is fast approaching.

A young, small plant can go straight into the ground untrimmed. A larger plant may need to have any long or heavy bud-bearing stems trimmed back before planting. Handle the roots gently. Invert the container or growing bag, then cup the base of the plant in the palm of your hand to remove the container, leaving the roots and clinging soil uppermost. Observe the spread of the roots: they spread out at the sides more than down at the center.

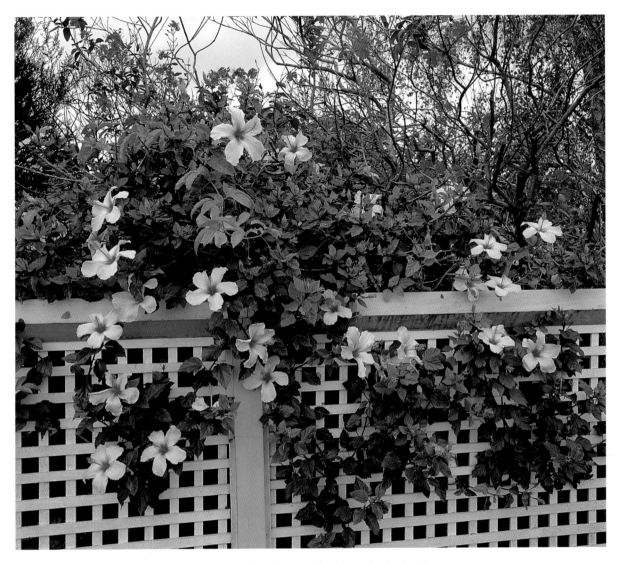

This hybrid has the support of a decorative lattice fence.

To accommodate this tendency, your planting hole should be wide and shallow, but well-dug and prepared deeply below, and mounded gently in the middle.

Plant your hibiscus so that the join of the base of the stem is at the same level of soil as before, i.e. the bole/collar area must be clear of the surface. It's especially important that grafted plants have the graft area kept clear of soil and mulch, so don't plant deeply. Remember that the shallow roots grow close to the surface. Cover lightly and press gently, then water well.

If you're transplanting a long-established in-ground hibiscus to a new location, it will be necessary to prune it first by cutting back to about two-thirds, perhaps more. It should be watered very thoroughly a day or two before transplanting. Have the new site well prepared before you attempt the move. Dig around the plant's base from the outer edge of the leaf drip-line, taking care not to cut the roots; if they do extend beyond where you dig, sever them cleanly. Dig from the sides down in stages, then work your fork under the shrub and lift it carefully. A fully-grown, mature hibiscus will have a correspondingly fully-grown root system, so its removal and relocation will need more than one person (preferably fully-grown but not necessarily mature!) to handle it. You'll need a sack or old rug under the roots for portability. Lower the shrub into its prepared new home, keeping the base of the trunk at the same level. Cover the roots, and water well.

Never feed a hibiscus immediately after planting – especially if you use chemical fertilizers – but give it a settling-in period first.

## Staking

The shallow roots of hibiscus are not deeply anchored. To stake or not to stake? That is the question only the gardener can answer, because the gardener knows better than anyone else if and where the winds blow. Is the site subjected to occasional storms? Regular sea breezes? Ripping westerlies? The worst winds of all are strong cold howlers that are dry rather than moist. No hibiscus hybrid can thrive if regularly subjected to these. Certain species though, rather than hybrids, are wind-tolerant (see Chapter 4).

The safest advice is to stake. And if in doubt, still stake. It's not just anchorage that's the concern. A hibiscus blown over by the wind may have its roots injured and, if damage is severe, root rot can set in. Hardwood stakes are best. Bang them into place *before planting* and use soft ties to hold the stem. Never use hard twine or wire or any material that can wound.

If you've found a spot up against a wall, or well-sheltered by overhang and surrounded by dense foliage, or in the niche of a recessed pocket, or other such special place, you may not need to stake. Or you may have trellising, or banks of boulders – it all depends on the site. Or you may be blessed with a

Raised beds ensure drainage and allow for quality controlled soil.

climate that is always calm – a real rarity – so that your hibiscus need no buttressing. Obviously, because low-growing hibiscus are a lot less prone to damage, selecting plants that don't grow very tall is a wise preventive measure in windy areas.

*Footnote on cultivation:* These are optimum provisions, but of course it's not always possible to give each hibiscus the perfect environment. Witness those other hibiscus, those other tenacious shrubs out there in odd spots, on roadsides and cliffs, by streams and abandoned homes, in gardens long neglected – sprawled or stunted, ragged or overgrown, they still unfurl their petals to the sun, such is their will to survive.

CHAPTER 3

# *Container Culture*

Tropical hibiscus adapt well to container growing because of their shallow rooting systems and container plants are especially versatile in confined areas. For people who move house a lot or for apartment dwellers who garden on balconies, potted tropical hibiscus can be exhibited at their best and at other times removed to obscurity. For those who live in very cold climates, containers are indispensable. The cultivation of potted tropical hybrids in climates where they must be over-wintered indoors is the subject of Chapter 9.

## Types of containers

Select containers that are as wide as they are deep, or even wider. Width is necessary because the plant's fine feeder roots spread out from the base of the stem like spokes of a wheel, almost horizontally. There are more of these roots than there are anchoring ones growing downwards. A tall, narrow container is therefore unsuitable.

Plastic pots are fine, although in very warm climates they may heat up and harm the roots, and it is important to avoid one side of the pot heating up while the other shaded side stays cool. A safer arrangement in very hot areas might be to put plastic pots inside outer pots.

Some professional hibiscus growers recommend clay-fired pots rather than plastic because unglazed terracotta pots "breathe". Containers made of stone

or concrete can also be used. Timber too is an excellent material for accommodating hibiscus if it is the moisture-durable kind, like cedar, and wooden wine barrels, are wonderful.

A large containered hibiscus can be heavy. If you're a pot-shuffler with a yard full of plants, and you spend your time and back-bending strength moving them, consider purchasing a gardener's trolley or appliance trolley.

Above right: Bred for indoor culture, this 'Burnaby' series hybrid has been trained as a standard.
Opposite: One of the 'Burnaby' series, this standard hibiscus makes a splash of indoor color.

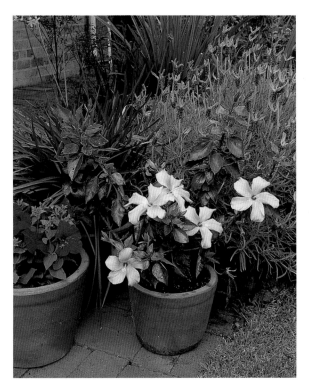

In small gardens containers can be arranged according to flowering times and effective color schemes. Then, when flowering is over, the plant can be moved.

While potted hibiscus may be heavy, their growth habit is gentle. Unlike vigorously rooted plants overdue for repotting or for planting out, hibiscus roots never burst their confines.

Orchids, fleshy-rooted agapanthus, shrubs, bulbous plants, and many others with expansive or exploratory roots can crack open a container. By contrast, when hibiscus roots reach their limit they start to suspend growth. As they reach the pot's perimeter they turn and grow down the sides before only slowly starting to fill up the center.

You can see this for yourself if you examine one that has been potted for a few months. Shake it free of potting mix to observe the shape of the roots forming a mound over a central cavity. Only when all the outer areas of the container are occupied will the roots start to fill the middle.

## Size

For a medium hibiscus (to 6 ft/2 m), a good-sized container to start with is one with a diameter at the top of 12-24 in (30-60 cm), tapering to a little narrower at the base, with the height of the container about the same as the width. You can grow hibiscus in pots wider than higher, but not the reverse, because a tall narrow size is wasted at the bottom and too restricting at the top, so start with a 12-16 in (30-40 cm) size, and after several years repot to a larger one.

## Drainage

Drainage holes should be in the outer rim of the base of the pot, rather than underneath – or both – because matted roots underneath can in time clog up drainage, and will certainly do so with pots standing in saucers – a good reason for raising pots on small blocks. Saucers have their uses in indoor culture and during times of absence when you are not there to water frequently. At such times shallow saucers can be left with water, which also helps cooling in excessively hot weather. In general though, since sharp drainage is essential, hibiscus grown in pots need side drainage and regular watering.

## Potting mix

Because of the need for a mix with high air-filled porosity, as explained on page 17, your potting mix should always contain some sand. The best sand to use is "sharp" sand, which refers to the surface of the individual grains. Sand composed of sharp rather than rounded grains usually comes from granite and is better at providing air-filled porosity.

The mix must be friable and loose. A combination of 80 percent potting mix (usually fine pine bark) and 20 percent sand is quite standard; or you can use a 50-50 blend of high-quality garden loam and commercial potting mix with the sand. You can add a small quantity of well-aged compost to the potting mix (making sure it has no worms in it

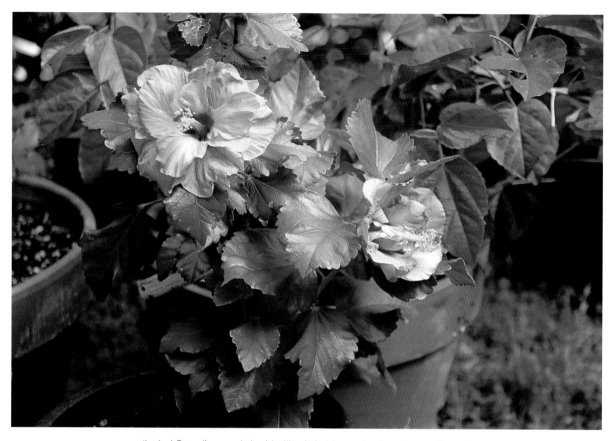

'Isobel Beard', a semi-double lilac hybrid growing in a terracotta pot.

because worms block drainage), or a small scoop of fine peat, in addition to the sand. A soilless mix contains no trace elements, which can be supplied through slow or medium-release fertilizer. It is best if some compost is used in every mix, in small amounts only – or else applied as a surface mulch. Well-rotted manure can also be used as a covering mulch.

## Plant selection

Always select compact and bushy hibiscus for growing in pots, avoiding especially plants that are scraggy, or tall and leggy. Although pruning can control size, it is best to buy a smaller bush at the start, preferably one with a thick branching habit and plentiful foliage.

## Planting

Fill your container about a third full and gently position the hibiscus in place, taking care not to compress or damage the roots. Do not plant too deeply. Keep the join of roots and stem close to the surface. Add the rest of the mix to fill up the pot, then lightly pat down to leave a space of about 1-1½ in (3-4 cm) at the top. Never fill right to the top. Water well. Once the plant has settled in the level may drop slightly and you can apply a thin layer of mulch. Mulching is beneficial but not essential.

## Feeding and watering

If you use slow-release fertilizer in the form of coated granules or pellets, you may need to feed your hibiscus with these twice a year – once in spring and again in early fall. In a cool climate and with small plants, once a year may be sufficient. If you

1: A newly rooted cutting, showing white, healthy roots.

2: Potted and after several more weeks, both foliage and roots show robust growth.

3: Typical root growth. At this stage the young plant can be repotted to a larger container, although this is not yet necessary.

4: By now the roots have encased the mix in a thick mesh wrapping and are starting to fill the center. It is time to repot.

5: Before placing the plant in the new pot, gently tease out the bottom roots to encourage them to spread.

6: When filling the new container with mix it is important to keep the stem/root join at the same depth: do not bury it deeper than the previous level. Staking is recommended.

use a liquid foliar spray, feeding will be more often – once every two or three weeks during the growing season.

As for watering, water only when your hibiscus needs it. How do you tell? Scratch the surface to a depth of about ³/₄-1 in (2-3 cm): if the potting mix is moist, don't water; if it is dry, give it a thorough hosing. Always water well after feeding.

## Maintenance and pruning

How big will your potted hibiscus grow? Exactly as big as you want it to. The size of the pot controls the size of the plant. In a 12-24 in (30-60cm) diameter (and height) container, a hibiscus will grow to a maximum of 5 ft (1.5 m) high from the base of the pot, and will be about 39-51 in (1-1.3 m) across – which is probably as large as any gardener can handle. In fact, a smaller size may be preferred.

If you do prefer a smaller bush, just prune it. Not every gardener realizes that as you trim your foliage, your plant will self-prune its roots. It works like this. Suppose you reduce your shrub to about 20 in (50 cm). The reduction in foliage will trigger the retraction of the feeding roots down inside the soil. As they retract they leave tiny tunnels of air in the mix, like worm tunnels but narrower. The roots will react in this way whether it is a container plant or a large bush growing in the ground where the spread of feeding roots extends out to the leaf drip-line, so that the outer dimensions of the bush determine the outer limits of the roots.

During this time of root reduction it is imperative that you do not feed the hibiscus. The retracting roots are not capable of taking up nutrients; they are well provided for with air from the air tunnels they leave, while the plant at this time draws upon its own store of carbohydrates. So when radical pruning results in a surge of new growth, that growth comes from the stored energy of the plant, not from nutrients in the soil.

Trimming the bush to trim the roots is a wonderfully neat system for the home gardener. Although you can repeat the procedure as a reliable way of keeping a containered hibiscus in shape for years, it will eventually need fresh medium and rejuvenation. The color of the roots is a good indicator of general health: white roots are robust, while darker roots are often a sign of poor condition. When you repot, pot to the next size only.

## Repotting

You'll know when it is time to repot if the roots have grown through the drainage holes and the plant's appearance indicates that it has used up all the available nutrients and is ready for a fresh feed. Repot to the next size by removing – carefully – the root-bound plant and placing it in the potting mix in the new container with the stem join at the same level. Unlike other root-bound plants that respond well to having their matted roots teased out, hibiscus tolerate only very gentle handling of their roots.

## Containers in garden planning

The main advantage of container culture is of course portability, but there is also the useful option of using containers for visibility or invisibility. Garden designers suggest planting decorative or eye-catching pots with plain or unassertive foliage plants

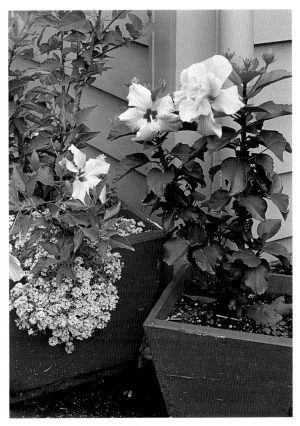

Blue containers offer color contrast here, with yellow double 'Crown of Bohemia'.

that don't compete for attention, and conversely, planting plain pots with dramatic or very floriforous plants. This rule works well for hibiscus. Shrubs grown in dull pots can show off their flowers to full effect; then, in the off-season when there is only foliage and the hibiscus may look quite drab, the plain pot can be put inside a larger, more decorative outer pot. Interest then focuses on the container.

The strategy of hiding a plain container when the hibiscus is flowering at full throttle is just as useful. The pot can be quite invisible in the garden. Any bushy or clumping plants – annuals, perennials or shrubs, even large bulbs and grasses – can hide a pot or two. The advantages of being able to site a hibiscus in such places is the reason many gardeners grow them only in pots.

# CHAPTER 4

# Hibiscus in Cool Climates

## Hybrid hibiscus

In general, tropical hibiscus hybrids can cope with temperatures down to 37°-39° F (3° or 4°C.) In extremes, when a drop in temperature down to 32°F (0°C) or below is short, sharp and doesn't linger, healthy hibiscus will pull through. Prolonged periods of near-freezing temperatures are borderline conditions and can be fatal. But take heart – there are strategies for dealing with cold.

If you live in a climate with fiercely cold winters, the only way to keep hibiscus alive is to grow them in pots and bring them indoors until spring. (See Chapter 9.) Of course, the best possible set-up is a conservatory. Failing that, a light sunny area such as an enclosed porch, conservatory extension or large bay window might offer accommodation. (It is through indoor gardening that you quickly learn the advantages bare flooring has over wall-to-wall carpet. Tiled floors or rugs and mats that can be lifted are the choice of most house-plant growers.)

Where winters are a little less severe, containered plants need not be taken indoors but can survive if moved to patios adjoining the house, to covered entranceways, garage walls, corner niches under the shelter of overhanging eaves, and other such places that provide protection from frost. This may be all that's necessary for your hibiscus to hibernate until spring; it may suffer a little from the chill (for evidence look for browning of the leaf margins, leaf drop, or, if actually frost-bitten, pulpy rather than hard stems) but will still revive in the new season. And remember, young plants are the most vulnerable – the older your hibiscus, the tougher it will be.

Foliar feeding with an organic liquid made from fresh seaweed is a proven promoter of frost resistance.

### Siting hybrids for winter protection

In some areas that are climatically marginal for hibiscus grown outdoors (i.e. where temperatures drop to freezing for short periods only), there are ingenious gardeners who have devized ways of helping their shrubs through winter. One garden, regularly subjected to quite heavy frosts, successfully accommodated a large hibiscus planted next to a recessed brick chimney. The fire, lit inside each night, would gradually warm the bricks, investing them with retained heat that was released during the day. The hibiscus appreciated its cosy nook and thrived. There is a great convenience in growing shrubs whose root systems are gentle and non-invasive. You can grow them close to drains and house foundations and need never worry.

Some growers advocate building barriers around plants growing in the ground. Barrier banks, which are much like tree wells, are surprisingly effective. To make them, mix soil with coarse organic material, such as shredded bark, pineneedles, leaf litter or wood-shavings. Then, using your hands to shape a mounded ring like a car tire but higher and smaller, encircle your hibiscus. You can use twigs,

Opposite: 'Southern Belle' hybrids of *Hibiscus moscheutos* will grow in climates with cold winters.

small branches or stakes to strengthen the structure. The barrier can be as high as you can make it, up to 20 in (50 cm), but must be clear of the base of the trunk. This is especially important if the hibiscus is grafted, for the graft needs air circulation around it. By acting like a quilt insulating the sleeping occupant, a barrier bank can help protect the stem, the lower part of the bush, and the ground surface area from the extremes of wind and frost.

Another way of dealing with light frost is to cover your plants with burlap or sacking laid over a temporary structure. Fibrous, natural materials seem to be more effective than synthetic windbreak cloth; plastic should never be used.

Tall stakes can form the framework, which needs to be well clear of the foliage so that there is no contact. Of course, in areas with cold temperatures and cold wet soil, it is assumed that your hibiscus already have the advantage of raised beds.

The combination of these defenses – an elevated site and temporary winter cover, as well as some protective mounding around the base – can carry a healthy hibiscus through the grimmest of winters.

Even without these precautions, hibiscus will survive if only lightly touched by frost. The leaves will be burned, but in spring new growth will shoot away.

### Pruning frost-damaged plants

There's a temptation to trim off frost-burned leaves immediately because they are unsightly. Don't! Never prune in winter. Never prune in cold weather. In any case, the shrub is likely to self-prune by shedding damaged leaves. Prune only when the weather has begun to warm up and there are signs of new growth. It is also advisable to feed several weeks before the pruning.

### Grafted plants

Grafting takes advantage of rootstock that has proved particularly robust or disease-resistant, and is used as a base for other, less vigorous or less resistant varieties. Some rootstock has proved to be more cold- tolerant than others, and these have been selected for growing in cooler climates. Cultivars grafted onto rootstock of 'Agnes Galt' and 'Suva Queen' have been highly successful, enabling these plants to grow in areas normally considered marginal or beyond the limits of hibiscus's range. Growers have also made much use of 'Albo-Lascinatus' as rootstock.

Gardeners in cooler climates growing hibiscus outdoors are advised to select only grafted plants. Local nurseries are the best source of advice about grafted selections for the local climate.

## Hardier hibiscus – other species

If you live in areas subjected to the full blast of winter, snow and all, you can still grow hibiscus in-ground outdoors. Three species, *Hibiscus syriacus*, *H. moscheutos* and *H. mutabilis* are fully cold-tolerant. Of these, the first two are available in hybrid form, bred for the commercial market and they are excellent plants for adding color to the garden; the third, *H. mutabilis*, does not hybridize.

Along with these three, there are other options for gardeners in cold regions. You can, of course, avoid winter problems altogether by growing tropicals in pots and bringing them indoors for the cold months (see chapter 9). Or you could try growing hibiscus annuals. Four lesser-known species that grow as annuals from seed are described here because of their novelty interest (two are edible) and because, more usefully, they dispense with the problem of over-wintering.

### Hibiscus syriacus and its hybrids

*H. syriacus* offers the gardener two things that *H. rosa-sinensis*-type hybrids cannot: cold-tolerance and the color blue. The flower color of the species is closer to lilac, but among the 40 or so worthy hybrids of *H. syriacus*, from a total of several hundred, there are a few with flowers in a rich blue.

*H. syriacus* has long been known throughout Asia, Europe, the Middle East, and the Mediterranean. There's evidence it has been cultivated since antiquity, and although research has established its origins as Asian (it is the national flower of Korea), early reports of the species growing in the Middle East resulted in the botanist Linnaeus mistakenly referring to it as "Syrian"– hence "syriacus".

In cultivation it has proved to be long-lived, tough, and well-adapted to dry climates and to prolonged drought. It is frequently used as a backbone shrub in flower borders, and in the right climate makes an effective hedge. In form *H. syriacus* is more multiple branching, and (usually) more vase-shaped than the warm-climate hybrids. The leaves are smaller and it is fully deciduous, although in the tropics it is sometimes semi-deciduous.

The flowers, sometimes likened to hollyhocks, are cup-shaped, and up to 6 in (15 cm) across. Some *H. syriacus* hybrids bear their blooms like bells. There are single, semi-double and double forms, and though smaller than the giant blooms of other hibiscus hybrids, their colors more than compensate: lilac and blue, mauve and maroon, magenta, pale pink and rose-pink, violet, purple and pure white. No yellow and orange here – these are the romantic colors of the boudoir: soft, sometimes powder-puffed, and almost always with a contrasting center of deep burgundy red.

Among recommended *H. syriacus* hybrids are: 'White Supreme' (white, semi-double), 'Ardens' (lavender-mauve, semi-double), 'Woodbridge' (wine-red, single), 'Carnation Boy' (lavender, double), 'Alba Plena' (pure white, semi-double), 'Hino Maru' (pure white, single), 'Coelestis' (violet streaked with wine, single), 'Lady Stanley' (soft pink, semi-double), 'Flying Flag' (white with red,

single), 'Double Wine' (exactly that), 'Rosalinda' (purple, semi-double), 'William Smith' (pure white, single), 'Heidi' (violet-blue, dwarf), 'Snowdrift' (white, semi-double), 'Ruber Plenus' (maroon-red, double), 'Mimihara' (cream/crimson, semi-double), 'Diana' (pure white, single), and 'Red Heart' (white with red veins and center, single). 'Blue Bird', developed in France with the name 'Oiseau Bleu', is the outstanding choice for a rich gentian-blue with purple center (single).

Common names for *H. syriacus* include Althea Rose and Syrian Rose, but the most widely used is Rose of Sharon. Elegant in name and in flower, its merits are many. With its preference for dry climates, it takes easily to cultivation in inland areas away

*Hibiscus syriacus*

*Hibiscus mutabilis* – The hibiscus flowers that change their colors.

from the sea (which is rare in the genus generally) while at the same time it grows well on the coast and tolerates salt air. Icy, frozen winters do not bother it, and many a bush emerges each spring from a blanket of snow. It is understandably popular in North American gardens (an ancient bush growing on Nantucket Island off the northeast coast of Massachusetts, U.S.A., testifies to its hardiness in conditions both snowy and saline), as it is in other continental climates that experience the extremes of heat and cold. The only climate in which it does not seem to thrive is one with year-round high humidity.

Cultivation requirements for this species are similar to those of other hibiscus. They prefer full sun, good drainage, water during the growing season, organic feeding, and their roots away from competition from other plants. They are similarly vulnerable to insect damage, particularly bud-boring beetles, but unlike hibiscus grown in mild sub-tropical climates where insects outlive the winter, *H. syriacus* grown in cold places outlive the insects. Like most hibiscus, they benefit from pruning, but should be pruned only in winter when bare of leaves. Cut them back resolutely by removing about half the bush; older bushes can be amputated even more. If not pruned, the shrub becomes unsightly and the flowers will be smaller. Pruning ensures health.

*H. syriacus* seem to grow best in the ground rather than in pots. A lack of trace elements, especially potassium and iron, has been suggested as the reason for their reluctant pot growth, in which case booster feeding of trace elements may help. With its hardiness to cold and drought, there's good reason to plant this species in the garden. It need never grow too big when controlled by pruning, and some cultivars have an ultimate height of only 39 in (1 m).

## Hibiscus mutabilis

Mutable means changeable, and the Latin "mutabilis" means undergoing change – which is exactly what the flowers of this hibiscus species do. They change color during the course of their brief life, starting off glistening white before becoming pale pink, then full, rich pink, and finally, as they begin to close, rose-maroon. All these colors are present on the bush at the same time – mutant magic.

Like *H. syriacus*, *H. mutabilis* is fully hardy and deciduous, or semi-deciduous in warmer climates. The leaves are impressively large. Downy and deeply cordate, from a distance they appear heart-shaped, and measure up to $5\frac{1}{2}$ in (14 cm) or more in length. They are borne on spreading branches which can sometimes grow almost horizontally if given the space, although pruning can modify the spread. The common name is Cotton Rose or Confederate Rose. This species produces flowers in both single and double forms, of which the delightful 'Plenus', a candyfloss double, is popularly grown. Their color change is renowned. Although the trait appears in other species and other hibiscus hybrids, nowhere is it as consistent and dramatic. Nor has this characteristic been transferred by blending with other species, since *H. mutabilis* appears to be genetically incompatible with all other hibiscus.

The novelty of the color change is the reason for growing it. In a small garden with space for only a couple of shrubs, one Confederate Rose can do the work of several. The change occurs both on and off the bush. An intriguing idea might be to invite guests to dinner and use the flowers for a table centerpiece, picking them early (the rate of change can be slowed by storing them in the refrigerator) and then watching the change – and the reaction of the diners – during the course of the meal.

The shrub is best grown in an open position without competition from other plants, especially without crowding from other foliage if you want the display to be seen at its best. The usual hibiscus feeding, moisture and drainage requirements apply, with feeding suspended in winter when the shrub is leafless.

Winter is the time to prune. *H. mutabilis* will grow into a small tree of 13-16 ft (4-5 m) in warm climates and if left unpruned, but a good height to maintain in a garden of modest proportions is about 8-11 ft (2.5-3.5 m). As with all hibiscus, pruning should be radical. There's a tendency for the dried fruiting capsules of *H. mutabilis* to remain after flowering and foliage have finished, so pruning by about half will rid the bush of these and ensure good growth in the following season. Hardwood cuttings taken during this winter prune can be propagated (see Chapter 8).

## Hibiscus moscheutos and its hybrids

*H. moscheutos* is a herbaceous perennial, i.e. it dies down each winter and comes up again in the spring. Hardy to temperatures well below freezing, its common name of mallow – mallow rose, swamp mallow, marsh mallow – indicates the type of conditions it favors in the wild. The name also describes the sweet confection, marshmallow. (The original ingredient that was mixed with sugar, gum arabic and egg white was the mucilaginous extract from the roots of the European marsh mallow, *Althaea officinalis*. Use of this species in medicines for coughs, burns and other ailments can be traced back to the ancient Greeks. It was this plant, not *H. moscheutos*, that the Greek physician and herbalist Dioscorides first named "hibiskos".)

*H. moscheutos* is one of several herbaceous perennial species, such as *H. militaris*, *H. coccineus* and *H. grandiflorus*, indigenous to the warm south-eastern states of the U.S. These have never been extensively cultivated as ornamental garden plants, but when hybridized they produced some real successes.

The first hybridizing took place about a century ago. It was followed in the 1950s by another program of hybridizing which built on the earlier work and culminated in the production of the brilliant series 'Southern Belle'. Today 'Southern Belle' is offered by seed merchants, along with the aptly named 'Dixie Belle', which is a dwarf form of 'Southern Belle', to gardeners around the world. Fresh seed germinates easily. It is also possible to acquire plants from cuttings if taken sufficiently early in the season to allow time for the tuberous roots to develop.

The outstanding feature of these hybrids is their flower size. On healthy, quality plants the size is staggering, for these blooms are giants, measuring as much as 12 in (30 cm) across. The color range within the two series of hybrids includes pink, white, crimson and several reds – all with deep maroon centers. Their swamp origins give them a huge advantage for gardeners with poorly-drained soil because they can tolerate wet roots in near-waterlogged conditions.

Here is a herbaceous, fully hardy, frost-tolerant perennial that will grow in situations with poor drainage, is usefully dormant in winter when you can forget all about it, shoots up in spring to grow vigorously to 3-6 ft (1-2 m), produces mammoth blooms in rich colors, and continues to do so year after year – all for the price of a packet of seeds. If these *H. moscheutos* hybrids are so marvelous, one might wonder, what's the catch? Why aren't they grown everywhere? There is no catch – only they do need a bit more care.

These hibiscus have tuberous root systems and, like all soft-stemmed perennials, their new spring shoots are tender and sappy; snails, slugs, and caterpillars love them. And they must be treated like soft-stemmed perennials and protected from injury; while other hibiscus make hardwood, *H. moscheutos* are like dahlias. Their huge flowerheads make them top heavy, and they are more prone than any other hibiscus to wind damage. They *must* be staked, and they *must* be protected from strong winds. They also need more water than other hibiscus. Given their swamp origins, it is not surprising that they can take

up a great deal of moisture during the growing season, but watering should be suspended in winter. Feed them over the summer, and watch for insects. Hygiene is important: any injured or damaged stems should be removed as these plants are especially vulnerable to disease. The plants should not be pruned – in late fall, as they shed their leaves, allow them to die back at their own pace. Only when the remaining stems have wilted to a brown color, rather than green, should you tidy up. Remaining stems can then be trimmed to a few inches above ground level and the area cleared of any debris that might harbor insects.

While it is true that they can keep going year after year and can be propagated quite easily from root division, some growers find that these herbaceous hybrids lose vigor after several seasons and choose to replace them with new plants grown from fresh seed.

*H. moscheutos* hybrids are not for windy climates. At 6 ft (2 m), 'Southern Belle' hybrids are taller than 'Dixie Belle' (3 ft/ 1 m) and have larger blooms, but both strains produce sumptuous flowers – flowers of such size that they are worth picking as a conversation piece. Both can be grown in pots but are much better in the ground where they can be included in mixed plantings and herbaceous borders. Massed plantings are spectacular. There is also a more recently bred strain called 'Mallow Marvels'.

The popularity of *H. moscheutos* hybrids has resulted in new breeding developments, with each year producing more new releases. Mass production means that these colorful plants are now cheaply available and sold even in supermarkets. Many people prefer to grow them only for one season, discarding the spent plants at the onset of winter. They then look forward to a new range of bold blooms to tempt them in the spring.

## Four species to grow as annuals

*Hibiscus trionum* is an annual or biennial native to many countries. A petite, unassuming little plant, it

The flowers of this 'Southern Belle' hybrid of *H. moscheutos* are among the largest of all hibiscus blooms. As a hardy, herbaceous perennial, 'Southern Belle' is dormant in winter.

grows a mere 20 or 24 in (50 or 60 cm), with very narrow, quite unhibiscus-like leaves and small decorative flowers. The flower's five petals, cream, yellow or sometimes white, surrounding a deep maroon center, are borne profusely in summer. They are short-lived, opening for just the duration of the warmest part of the day and closing in mid- to late afternoon.

Though inclined to be straggly, the soft-stemmed plant can make a contribution to the temperate perennial border, if mass planted. Being low growing, it needs no staking. In the sandy soils it enjoys it may become somewhat prostrate, while in richer soils it tends to grow more upright.

In the right conditions, *H. trionum* can grow so abundantly that it can almost be regarded as a weed by those fortunate enough to enjoy such a situation. Seed is not easily obtained, probably because the plant is so self-seeding, yet it is easy to grow and tolerant of most conditions.

As an annual *H. trionum* lends itself to gardens with frozen winters, to rock gardens, ornamental beds, and confined spaces in urban gardens. Like the species *H. insularis*, *H. trionum* is unspectacular but underrated.

*Hibiscus esculentus* (syn *Abelmoschus esculentus*) is a species grown mostly in the tropics, but will adapt to a cool climate as a summer annual. Give it the hottest spot you have (full sun, good drainage, moisture) and you'll be rewarded twofold. First, the plant (which grows to 6 ft/ 1.8 m) will bear flowers of an undeniably hibiscus hue, yellow with rich, dark wine centers and elongated staminal tubes; and second, if the summer and warmth last long enough, you can harvest the vegetable, okra. Okra is eaten in Asia, Africa and the U.S.A.'s southern states, where it is popularly used in gumbo. The younger the fruit is picked the better, so pick it when it is small, soft and mucilaginous, and try it in salads, or steamed

*Hibiscus trionum*, a low growing annual or biennial species.

and in soups. The flower buds and immature pods are also edible.

*Hibiscus sabdariffa*, easily identified by its bright burgundy-colored stems, is another tropical species that can be grown as an annual to produce both flowers and fruit. Like *H. esculentus*, the flowers are yellow with a deep red basal spot, but it is a more elegant plant, with blooms that are often a light primrose-yellow or suffused with pink that contrasts colorfully with the conspicuous red stems. When flowering has finished the remaining calyxes swell and turn bright red – they are edible and can be made into drinks, jellies and sauces. (See page 93 for the recipe.)

*Hibiscus manihot* (syn *Abelmoschus manihot*), a species from China, bears showy. Pale yellow or near-white

with dark brown centers, these are borne in clusters at the ends of the branches. The very large leaves are shiny, deeply-lobed and similarly handsome.

The one drawback to this quite sumptuous flower – apart from prickly seed capsules – is that it shares with most other species a short lifespan of less than a day. *H. manihot* is easily grown as an annual by raising from seed sown in late winter.

### Hibiscus diversifolius

This little-known and little-grown species, native to New Zealand and Pacific countries, won't survive more than a few degrees of frost. It grows to about 5 ft (1.5 m) and is inclined to spread. The stems are armed with small prickles and the leaves armed with hairs, while the flowers have the same pleasing color combination of many species: pale lemon petals arranged around a dark purple-red center. They are more bell-shaped than the hybrid flowers, remaining cupped rather than opening out fully.

*H. diversifolius* is useful for certain conditions as it tolerates damp and even swampy soils.

## *Alyogyne huegelii* (until recently *Hibiscus huegelii* but now reclassified)

A species with flower colors of exceptional beauty, this shrub is set apart from all the rest by its preference for dry conditions. Tolerant of light-to-moderate frosts, it is not for very cold climates unless the winter chill is offset by fiercely hot summers; but the so-called "desert hibiscus" is included in this list because it just might fit a problem dry climate where attempts to grow other hibiscus have failed.

*A. huegelii* will not grow in areas of high humidity. Although its roots need available moisture when young, once mature the shrub will cope with considerable drought, and indeed will flourish in really hot dry places – which is why it grows to perfection in Southern California.

And as for the flowers, they are delectable. The petals are arranged in an overlapped windmill format round a dark eye, and are usually lilac or purple; careful selection has produced some with deep blue flowers, hence the common name blue hibiscus. In the botanical gardens south of Newport Beach, California, where a formerly derelict area has come to life with massed plantings of one of the bluest of these, the effect is electrifying. In Californian residential gardens too, bright *A. huegelii* flowers set against the white background of Spanish-style houses make a splash of blue – pure pleasure.

*A. huegelii* is evergreen, has lobed, toothed and somewhat hairy leaves, and benefits from rigorous pruning after flowering to keep it compact, otherwise it tends to become straggly. It likes sandy soil, sharp drainage, full sun, and responds to light organic feeding. It is not long-lived and should be replaced every few years. Shunning humid climates, this species is the envy of many who can grow the

*H. syriacus* 'Elegantissima'

coastal hibiscus, so if you can give it the conditions it likes, cherish it.

## *Hibiscus arnottianus*

A half-hardy species that will grow in marginal areas that might be a touch too cold for hybrids, *H. arnottianus* comes from the mountains of the Hawaiian Islands where it grows at high altitudes and hence is more cold-tolerant. Its common name is Wilders White. Unlike other hibiscus, this one flowers on old wood, and is not pruned to produce or enhance flowering but only to tidy and shape.

*H. arnottianus* also has the attribute, unique to the genus, of scent. The perfume, though slight, is discernible on the single blooms that are long-lasting, white with pale pink veins and deep pink-red staminal tubes of striking length.

*Hibiscus diversifolius* bears modest flowers that are short-lived. But this species tolerates damp soils and poor drainage.

However, it is not for the flowers but for the roots that horticulturists have propagated *H. arnottianus*, because while the species does have some cold-tolerance, more importantly it is resistant to both root rot and borer, hence it has served as grafting understock for hybrids that lack this resistance. *H. arnottianus* has also been used extensively in hybridizing programs, with many of the marvelous cultivars of Hawaii owing their genetic heritage to this species.

This species likes high humidity, maximum sunlight, good drainage, and feeding and moisture as for other hibiscus, but not the pruning regime. If pruned, it may not flower the following season. By leaving it to grow at will, it can eventually become a small tree of 10-13 ft (3-4 m) – more in warm climates – although it is recommended that it be given a fairly severe pruning once every five years, and a light tip clipping every other year. It makes a handsome standard.

Not for very cold climates, *H. arnottianus* may be worth considering in areas with borderline winters. It can be propagated by seed sown in spring or by hardwood cuttings.

## Hibiscus relations for cooler climates

These are not true hibiscus but are Malvaceae members with hibiscus-like appearance.

*Alcea rosea* (syn. *Althaea rosea*), the enduring hollyhock, plant of the picket fence and chocolate-box paintings, is a biennial that thrives in cool climates – it is utterly, totally hardy – and is known for its spikes of cupped flowers. Easily grown in gardens with sharp drainage and full sun, and easily propagated from seed, the hollyhock is available in single and double forms in colors of the white-to-rose spectrum.

*Malva moschata*, the musk mallow, so-called because the leaves emit a musky scent when crushed, is another old species in cultivation for centuries. Native to Europe, including Britain, the musk mallow grows into a 3 ft (1 m) high branching perennial producing successive spires of mauvy white saucer flowers. 'Alba' is a white cultivar that grows to 3 ft (1 m) also. *M. moschata* is fully hardy.

*Malva sylvestris* is another hardy perennial, sometimes biennial. Erect to 3 ft (1 m), it bears hibiscus-like blooms in a range of colors from pure white to strong purple.

*Lavatera*, perhaps the most popular of all hardy Malvaceae ornamentals, includes the lovely sub-shrub *Lavatera cachemirica*, bearing silky pink flowers all summer; the perennial or annual *L. trimestris* 'Silver Cup', awash with pink flowers streaked with silver; and *L. trimestris* 'Mont Blanc', glistening with pure white pearls; but the outstanding performer is *Lavatera* 'Barnsley'. A newer, compact variety called *Lavatera* 'Lisanne' is also much admired. All are fully hardy.

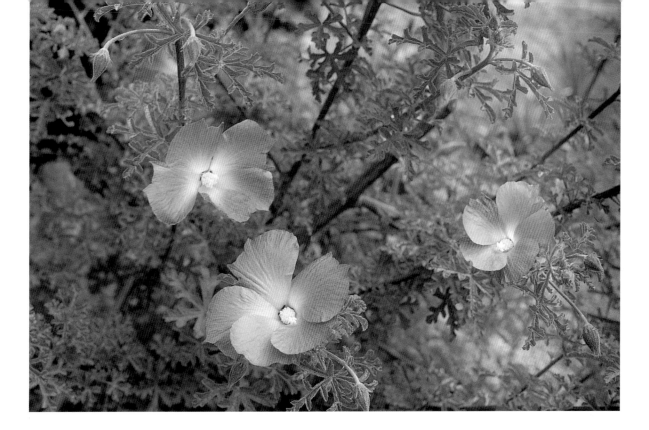

*Alyogyne huegelii* (formerly *Hibiscus huegelii*) has flowers in purple, mauve and occasionally quite blue, and tolerates dry climates and near-desert conditions.

*Sidalcea malviflora* and its cultivars are perennials with pink or rose flowers a little like the hollyhock. The clump-forming cultivar 'Jimmy Whittet' is recommended for perennial gardens. *Sidalcea* need full sun and drainage, and can tolerate the coldest of winters.

*Pavonia hastata* is evergreen and fully hardy. The deep maroon centers of these five-petaled flowers – in white, pink or pale mauve – make the plant very hibiscus-like. It can tolerate a little shade, likes rich, well-drained humus, and should be cut back hard in spring.

*Lagunaria patersonii*, the Norfolk Island hibiscus (Norfolk Island is 620 miles/1000 km north-west of New Zealand), is not fully hardy and tolerates only light frosts. In warm climates it grows into a tall pyramidal tree of 30-40 ft (9-12 m). The flowers are pale pink or rose- pink, with cream centers and five petals tapered at their outer edges. As a garden subject the Norfolk Island hibiscus has limitations, for the flowers are fairly small and the fast-growing tree fairly large; the main reason for growing *L. patersonii* is its tolerance of extreme coastal conditions.

*Abutilon*, the Chinese lantern or flowering maple, is a choice shrub. There are species and cultivars, and most are half-hardy. The ornate bell flowers in white, cream, yellow, orange, apricot, pink or red hang from upright or arching stems. In warm climates *Abutilon* grows best in part-shade, otherwise give it a sunny site well- protected from wind. Staking is recommended. One species which is hardier than most and well-suited to cooler climates is *Abutilon vitifolium* (syn *Corynabutilon vitifolium*), whose luscious, pale lilac- blue flowers, large and saucer-shaped, make it much admired and much sought.

## Indoor hybrids

Finally, if nothing else is possible, you can grow hibiscus hybrids indoors all year-round. Demand for warmth-loving hybrids by people living in less

*H. syriacus 'Leopoldii'*

hospitable climates led to some experimental tinkering whereby tropical hybrids were treated with hormonal growth retardant. The procedure was apparently first trialed in Canada and has since been copied in many countries, with the result that you can now buy a dwarf, fully-fledged flowering hibiscus that will grow indoors. This "new" plant resembles the outdoor shrubs in everything but an ability to mature, so it remains like a two-year-old seedling. It doesn't live long – it is not intended to, as producers can quickly sell you more. These potted specimens are released onto the market at about 1 ft (30 cm) high and wide, and grow to a maximum of about 20-24 in (50-60 cm), or to 3 ft (90 cm) if the pot is sited outside. Standardized versions are also available.

Opposite: A standard hibiscus creates an exotic indoor corner with other plants from warm climates.

Indoors the plant will bloom year-round if given maximum light. The less light it receives, the less foliage and flowers it will produce, and indoor conditions tend to produce dark leaves. Care involves the prevention of dust collecting on the leaves, for if its pores clog up the plant will sicken, so about once every two or three weeks the pot needs to be taken outside or into the bath and the foliage washed down. This will also prevent infestation from pests such as mites. In general these purpose-bred plants remain disease-free. They should be fed with slow-release fertilizer and watered regularly, especially immediately after feeding, and it is recommended that they not be repotted.

These dwarf indoor hibiscus flower in mostly single blooms in a variety of colors, and bring to the apartment dweller and cold-climate gardener a touch of the tropics they might otherwise be denied.

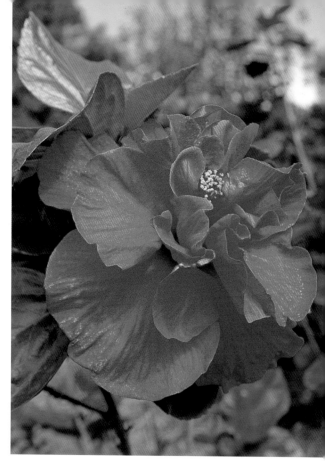

Above: The Chinese lantern, *Abutilon*, a hibiscus relation.
Below: 'Cinderella', also known as 'Burgundy Blush'.

Above: 'Satu'
Below: 'Mary Wallace'

Above: 'Norman Lee'
Below: 'Jack Clark'

Above: 'Saketani Blue', also known as 'Saketani Lavender'.
Below: 'White Fantasia', also known as 'Swan Lake'.

CHAPTER 5

# Hibiscus in Garden Design

Bold and imaginatively planned hibiscus gardens are – regretfully – rare. Perhaps that's because there used to be a prevailing belief that hibiscus had to be planted in beds separated from the rest of the garden; beds where each bush was evenly spaced at about 5 ft (1.5 m) apart, and destined to remain the exclusive territory of hibiscus alone, forbidding entry to any other plant. Such gardens can be very boring. Blobs of uniformly spaced bushes can look a lot like civic park displays or trial beds, and not much like the kind of leafy retreat most people seek to create in their backyards.

By all means grow them this way if you wish, but do realize that it is not the only way. A fresh approach is easily gained by visiting gardens designed by professional landscapers. Professionals spend a lot of time working through the whole plan, of which plant selection is only a small part. They consider every aspect of climate and topography, of views and existing or "borrowed" (i.e. neighboring) landscapes, of buildings, boundaries, entrances, soil, drainage, light, shade and sun … all this in close consultation with clients. The finished design will show axis lines and focal points, include vertical and horizontal dimensions, and take into account the garden's form, depth, texture and use of color.

All this may sound complex, but the aim is simplicity. The most successful gardens are often very simple. The secret lies in unifying materials and

plants, so that instead of mixing, for example, stone, timber, paving, concrete, and brick, only one material is used throughout. It is the same with plants. Instead of planting one of this and one of that, the skilled designer selects a favorite with good form, foliage and blooms – and then plants lots of it. Repetition unifies and strengthens the structural elements and overall plan. Twenty different hibiscus in 20 different colors does not make for good design. The selection must be narrowed down. Yes, it may be difficult to choose just one hibiscus from all those delectable hybrids you've already shortlisted to a mere eight or nine (you want them all!) but there will still be a place for the others as secondary features supporting the star performer.

Planning is all-important. The smaller your garden, the more essential it is to plan on paper. Money paid for professional advice is money well spent. A tight, tiny space at the rear of an inner-city apartment is exactly the sort of place that benefits most from landscaping expertise. Conversely, a large rural property may have less need of such input because it will already have areas allocated by fencing and hedges for crops, for edible gardens, pet animals, groves of natural forest, and so on. So if you garden within close confines, and especially if you're starting a new garden from scratch, consider consulting a designer. If you cannot afford one – and cannot afford to wait until you can – buy or borrow books on garden design. They can trigger ideas.

On the other hand, it should be said too that, while most gardeners delight in design – just as most people apply some sort of aesthetic rigor to choosing furnishings, or clothing, or pictures to hang on walls

Opposite: Hibiscus make attractive border subjects planted with perennials and shrubs, as this white flowering, cold-tolerant, *Hibiscus syriacus* hybrid shows.

Hibiscus and sea – always an appealing combination.

– there will always be collectors for whom disciplined layout is irrelevant. These are the gardeners who know every species in the genus, who never turn down a chance to add and expand, who can relate anecdotes for every find, who encourage rampant self-seeding, and whose plant knowledge is always deep and often scholarly. Such gardeners and gardens have much to offer, and should be valued. But for most hibiscus growers, some guidance will be helpful.

## Some landscaping suggestions

### Fire and water

The most dramatic backdrop you can give hibiscus is a seascape. As coastal plants, their affinity with the sea shows to great advantage in beach gardens where they can frame a sea view. Lucky the gardener who can grow a vivid 'Big Tango', 'Red Robin', 'Mollie

Cummings' or some other sublime hybrid fired from a red furnace to contrast with a sheet of blue.

If you cannot command a sweep of ocean, or a chink of inlet, then even a slender gleam of silvery gray beyond the ridge can bring together these two opposing elements of energy and calm – and of course a swimming pool or water feature will have the same effect.

### A solid background

A wall may be a more attainable backdrop. In cool climates the sheltering, warmth-collecting properties of a high, solid wall can make the difference between growing hibiscus and not growing them. For centuries, northern hemisphere gardeners have used south-facing walls to nurture plants that would otherwise not thrive. A wall has practical and aesthetic value. If it lacks the pleasing appearance of stone or brick – the more ancient, the

Above: The painted blue background, which offsets the glowing red hibiscus flowers, echoes the role of blue sea; and by limiting the hybrid choice to just one and repeating it, the result is simple but stunning.

Left: An entranceway gives protection in cooler climates and these hardy potted hibiscus offer a colorful greeting for visitors.

more the appeal – it may well be paintable. Paint can work wonders. Paint a background to display your dazzling hibiscus: perhaps olive green or dark forest green, or brown, or various lighter, neutral shades. Or you could splash out and try a rich blue. In confident hands strong purple can work magic. And in a courtyard garden, especially one with contemporary architecture, try white – in classic Grecian Isle style, white never fails as a foil for potted hibiscus.

Alternatively, clothe your walls in living greenery. Self-clinging vines can cover a fence or wall so densely that the underlying structure is invisible. Ivy is an obvious example, although it is

Opposite top: These extra-tall, container-grown standards have been grafted twice: first, onto other rootstock, then the "head" onto the "stem". But this treatment is not needed to grow a successful standard.
Bottom: A newly clipped hedge of 'Andersonii'.
Right: 'Albo-Lascinatus' grown over an archway.

not to everyone's liking and can be too tenacious. *Ficus pumila* (Zone 8) is as dense as ivy and a better alternative. The rich flowers of *Campsis radicans* (Zone 6) match the fiery color range of hibiscus so the self-clinging vine can be both backdrop and color coordinator. Climbers that sprawl and send out long arms and tentacles are not recommended, but there are many others that are less obstructive. *Senecio macroglossus*, the wax vine (Zone 10), needs some control but is not rampant; *Hoya* species are gentle climbers and trailers, although they prefer shade; *Manettia luteo rubra* (Zone 10) from South America is very moderate in habit, *Rhodochiton atrosanguineus* (Zone 10) even more so; *Parthenocissus quinquefolia* (Zone 4) is the self-clinging Virginia creeper famed for its deciduous foliage; *Schizophragma* (Zone 6) is also self-clinging; and the hardy silverlace vine *Polygonum aubertii* (Zone 4) is of easy culture. Other choices might include the half-hardy ornamental grapes or the ever-popular wisterias, which tolerate the coldest of winters (Zone 5).

Worries about the roots of climbers robbing nutrients from hibiscus territory can be solved by planting the vine on the other side of the wall or fence and encouraged to grow to the top and spread over the sunny side. In any case, most vines send down deeper roots than the shallow-feeding ones of hibiscus. Except in cold climates, upwardly mobile plants do best with their base in the shade and their upper levels in sun, so by positioning them on the cool side of the wall both climber and hibiscus benefit.

## Hedges of tropical hibiscus

Hibiscus hedges are undervalued as structural components in garden design. As a shrub grown almost exclusively for its flowers, it is not surprising that its use as a foliage bush has been ignored. Yet within the huge range of hybrids that offer every kind of leaf size, shape and texture, as well as form and habit of branching, there are some with such handsome foliage that they can be grown for this alone. Regular clipping enhances and encourages the foliage quality. The cultivar 'Andersonii' is one of the best for this purpose. It is a tough, tolerant grower with small scarlet blooms that in a sprawling, unpruned bush tend to be pendulous, but on a clipped hedge are borne close to the foliage, that has the additional attraction of producing fresh new growth with a bronze tinge.

So consider growing a hibiscus hedge. It will make a bold framework, as well as providing a perfectly matched backdrop for other hibiscus. However, discipline will be needed. A short, half-hearted hedge is not worth bothering about. Make it long and strong or not at all. It will also take discipline to shear it regularly of all those attractive flowers (though you can collect them up and fill a bowl) but your efforts will be well-rewarded.

To plant a low hedge the spacing needs to be about 27 or 31 in (70 or 80 cm) apart. A high hedge, up to 8ft (2.5 m) high, will need a spacing of about 3-4 ft (1-1.3 m), and a higher hedge even more. Ensure that the individual plants are of the same size and in good health before you plant; rather than dig and prepare separate holes for each plant, it is better to dig a trench for extra drainage and for filling with extra compost.

## Pleached hibiscus hedges

A variation on hedge-growing is pleaching, which means intertwining by encouraging branches of closely spaced trees or shrubs to grow together. The word comes from the Old French *plessier*, meaning to twist or to plait. When combined with trimming, the method produces a hedge with an intricate branch structure on a free-standing row of clear trunks. Horticulturally, it has a long history dating from Tudor England when pleached avenues were a status symbol indicating the number of gardeners a landowner could afford; artistically, it is a classic design form widely admired.

To pleach hibiscus a strong and well-constructed framework is needed until the row is fully established. The main staking posts for each trunk must be driven into the ground before planting, and they must be as high as the intended finished hedge. Spacing between the posts will be about 5-6 ft (1.7-2 m). Horizontal wires, tightly stretched, form the framework to which the lateral branches are tied. Laterals are encouraged to grow in a flat plane, while any wayward shoots appearing on the trunk or elsewhere are pinched out. Once a densely woven screen has been established it can be clipped and maintained like an ordinary hedge.

Certain tropical hybrids make better pleached hedges than others. Those which make good standards are best. The cultivar popularly called 'Ruth Wilcox', correctly named 'Albo-Lascinatus',

grows well when pleached, or when grown as an overhead arch or an arbor. To a lesser extent the species *H. schizopetalus* can be used this way. Both *H. schizopetalus* and 'Albo-Lascinatus' are less hardy than the reliable 'Andersonii' mentioned above.

## Other foliage uses

For a foliage-only shrub that is visually arresting, try growing the cultivar with variegation, 'Snow Queen'. At a distance it shimmers. Close up, the ice-white leaves show much more white than green, making a splendid foil for the scarlet blooms (although these flowers are not the reason for growing this variety). Give it a position of prominence, such as a stand-alone bush – kept well-shaped by pruning – maybe at the far end of a path or walkway. If possible, site it in part shade, for filtered sun heightens the effect.

'Cooperii' is an earlier hybrid with variegated foliage, but its performance is surpassed by 'Snow Queen'. Another, with tri-colored foliage in green, white and pink, is 'Rose Flake'. For a purple-foliaged effect, try growing the species *H. acetosella*, known as the "false rosella plant", a species with remarkably plum-colored leaves and plum-colored flowers to match. *H. glaber* 'Purpurea' has similarly-tinted foliage, while the hybrid 'Andersonii' bears leaves with a bronze-red sheen.

## Standards

Unless you're an experienced grower, it is probably more convenient, and certainly faster, to buy a ready-made standardized hibiscus than to create your own. But standards come at a price. The high cost reflects the time that went into the process of training a straight stem upwards to be topped off with a crown of foliage, as well as the expertise that went into the grafting of that stem, although not all standards are necessarily grafted. Hybrids that make good standards on their own roots include 'Pink Psyche', 'Albo-Lascinatus', 'Sprinkle Rain', 'Sylvia Goodman', and the white form of 'Fantasia'.

To grow your own, you'll need a clump of young

Above: In this narrow bed, the hibiscus hybrids are kept low with regular pruning.
Left: 'Snow Queen' – a hybrid with the unusual combination of bright red blooms borne on white variegated foliage.

plants packed closely together in enough shade to make them head up in search of light. This takes time. As they grow, monitor them and remove side growth as soon as it appears, and keep them staked. Select the most vigorous of them as your specimen standard, but keep them together to prevent branching. Aim for a final height of 5 ft (1.5 m), possibly taller, and then encourage branching and leaf growth by giving them space and sunlight. A good shape is obtained by very frequent light clipping, which is kept up until the "head" has reached the shape and size you want. Some designers claim that the ideal proportion to aim for is a plant with a crown width that is half the height of the stem.

If you're not concerned with cost, or with the challenge of growing your own, you can ask a

The lower branches of this mature hibiscus have been removed to keep it from cluttering the picket fence.

specialist grower to custom-make you a standard of your choice, for there are hundreds of hybrids that can be made into respectable standards. The selection at retail garden centers will be more limited.

Once you've got your standard, take care with its placement in the garden: make it a focal point. Be wary of windy sites because the stake to which the standard is tied may be thinner than normal, to keep it from being conspicuous. If you plan to grow your standard in-ground, you'll need to have prepared the site in advance. If you keep it in its container (and often such a quality plant is packaged in a quality container), take your time experimenting with the site so that it will give maximum impact. Visual impact is, after all, the reason for sculpturing plants. Feed and water it as you would any hibiscus, but give closer attention to keeping it in its intended shape.

## Espaliered hibiscus

Generally, hibiscus do not lend themselves to being espaliered in the classic manner of those ancient and gnarled pear trees grown in Northern Europe. Pear and apple branches frequently grow at right angles and, compared with hibiscus, will "set" themselves this way for ever. In contrast, hibiscus stems remain pliable, so espaliering them may be only partially successful. You'll need a fairly straight main-stemmed variety with strong side shoots (such as 'Rose Scott' or 'General Corteges'), and you'll need wires and tying twine, and plenty of patience. The pliable stems allow them to be bent without snapping so that in time they should stay where you want them to. It is not for beginners.

## Hibiscus in garden beds

The advice given in the past, to plant evenly spaced hibiscus bushes in their own beds, undoubtedly benefited the hibiscus but may not have benefited the homeowner. Not only is such expansive sunny space rare in the contemporary urban garden that often serves to provide privacy and seating and entertaining areas in a narrow plot at the rear of the house, but it is hardly an inspired design. The aesthetics of design need to be worked through in conjunction with the garden's functions.

If open space is limited to a central area or courtyard assigned for seating, the surrounding area will be most efficiently and effectively utilized if it is raised. Terracing and step-down levels can be ideal for hibiscus, for several reasons. A series of raised levels that at the highest might be 3-5 ft (1 to 1.5 m) above the original ground level will, firstly, allow the plants growing there to receive more sun; and secondly, guarantee good drainage. It will also enable you to get the best soil mix at the start and be more accessible for maintenance. By planting at different levels, closer spacing is possible, and visually, the vertical view, with flower and texture interest at varying levels (that means the least attractive part of hibiscus bushes, the base, will be concealed by surrounding shrubbery), gives structure and enhancement to the whole garden. Such elevated planting screens neighbors, too.

Blocks, bricks, railroad ties, timber edging, logs, and of course stone and natural large rocks all make good structures. On a modest scale, height can be gained at only 20 in (50 cm) or so by placing large containers on the higher level. Better still, remove the bottoms of the containers and partially bury them as permanent fixtures, so that they themselves become miniature raised beds. Remember that the planting area for hibiscus need only be 15 in (38-40 cm) diameter.

## Companion plants

If you garden on one level and want to mix other ornamentals with hibiscus, the trick is to select plants whose roots either don't penetrate deeper than the surface mulch, such as the ground covers suggested below, or that go much deeper. Most trees are obviously excluded. Palms, though, with their tidy root balls, are ideal, and small, non-invading shrubs can always be grown close by hibiscus if you plant your hibiscus on minimally-raised edging or mounds.

Ground-covering plants can fulfil the role of a living mulch, helping to keep the ground moist and weed-free. As well as an aid in stabilizing the surface soil and as a temperature buffer for hibiscus, ground covers help maintain a consistent acidic level. During times of drought they are also useful indicators of moisture levels because they'll start to wilt in time to alert the gardener of the need to water. And of course, ground covers are a lot more attractive than bare soil or mulch. Suitable plants include *Viola hederacea*, *Ajuga*, *Ophiopogon*, especially the all-tolerant *O. japonicus*, and *O. planiscapus* 'Nigrescens', also the flowering garlic *Tulbaghia violacea*, and *Tradescantia pallida* 'Purple Heart'.

Epiphytes hold little threat for hibiscus and can make successful companion plants, as well as having

Above: Color and texture – while the hibiscus colors blend beautifully with the paving below and the brick wall behind, there is striking textural contrast with the succulents in the foreground.

Below: *H. syriacus* 'Heidi'

Hibiscus and palms bring to the entrance of this cottage-style house and trellis arch an unexpectedly tropical appearance. The soft lemon hibiscus on the right is especially pleasing when surrounded with foliage plants.

rainforest appeal. Bromeliads planted around hibiscus may need to be selected for sun tolerance. Orchids, too, might find a home in pockets of small logs and stumps positioned to receive filtered sunlight.

Perhaps the most reliable of companion plants are annuals. Hibiscus grow happily in close company with anything temporary, and annuals are not there for the long-term. Massed plantings grown from seed or put in as seedlings can be fed and cared for – and then discarded at the end of the season. Colors can be chosen to blend or contrast with hibiscus – blended colors may be more successful – and foliage that doesn't detract should be used. This means choosing mid-textured foliage that is neither very large nor very fine.

## Color

The hibiscus color spectrum widens with every new hybrid released into cultivation, but it is strongest in the yellow-orange-red-pink portions, thinning out at the purple-lilac edge, with two marked exceptions: the species *Alyogyne huegelii*, formerly *Hibiscus huegelii*, of which there are forms in deep blue; and *H. syriacus* and its hybrids, which are almost exclusively in the purple-blue range. Of course, there are plenty of white and pale pastel hybrids.

Strong colors are best grouped together. Clear yellow and yellow-orange hibiscus go well with marigolds. (Don't dismiss familiar faces for their commonness; undemanding culture frees up your time to spend on hibiscus and other plants.)

The choice of color of both painted background and of hibiscus are clearly intentional – and very successful.

Sunflowers, *Zinnia*, *Tagetes*, *Calendula*, and *Rudbeckia* come in these shades, as does the gleaming *Eschscholzia* (Californian poppy). Red, apricot and pink hibiscus can be similarly matched. Nasturtiums are good for attracting aphids away from hibiscus, as well as for their hibiscus colors. Perennials include *Geum*, *Gerbera*, *Anigozanthos*, *Kniphofia*, and the outstanding *Hemerocallis* (daylily) whose galaxy of new cultivars allows you to color-match your hibiscus with precision.

When thinking about color, don't confine yourself to flowers but give as much, or even more, attention to foliage. Ivy-leaf geranium, for example, can be a better way of tying colors together in a hibiscus garden, especially in wine-red shades. And look also beyond plants. Look to the colors already existing in the garden by assessing (the merits or otherwise of) the colors of containers, statues and ornaments, seats, tables, fences, walls, tool sheds and utility areas, gates … all of these should be considered as part of your canvas.

It is regrettably true that fashion frequently dictates not only to the retail market but to gardeners' plant-buying decisions – however firmly resolved the will to resist – and flower colors are a good example.

When Vita Sackville-West created her white and silver garden at Sissinghurst it was a stroke of genius, but all those copies that sprouted in the 1970s eventually became tiresome, which is why strong colors took hold in the 1980s and 1990s. Perhaps now is the time to revisit white. Perhaps a fresh

Right: A number of elements are used in this
contemporary design: curves contrasted with the
perpendicular palm, rounded foliage, dark greens against
pale walls, and the pleasing effects of a pastel palette.

version, a white and cream garden centered around
hibiscus, could lead the way to new ideas. A few
luminous blooms of 'The Bride', 'Great White', or
'White Piccardy' might be surrounded with mass
plantings of that white-leafed hibiscus 'Snow
Queen', grown strictly for the foliage, and contrasted
with large-leafed, strongly formed foliage plants.
Perhaps the red flowers of 'Snow Queen' could lead
to a red and white theme. And another idea: fiery
orange-red on a green background could be achieved
by planting masses and masses of foliage plants with
large leaves of high luster and setting against this the
ember glow of a hybrid such as 'Fire Engine' or 'Big
Tango'. The temptation to include other species or
even similar hibiscus varieties would have to be
resisted, but in compensation would be the freedom
to splash out on a host of foliage plants. There's
plenty of scope for experiment. All of these themes
can be achieved with hibiscus in containers by
placing the hibiscus in front of in-ground plants.

## Themes

Whatever the theme of the garden, the extent of its
success is the extent to which it is carried through:
that means resisting the urge to plant things that are
not part of the plan. Hibiscus are versatile and can
adapt to all sorts of treatment. The smaller-flowered,
denser-foliaged ones lend themselves more to
shaping and to the standards associated with formal
gardens, while the big blowsy blooms belong to a
less-structured, highly floriferous theme. Rainforest
themes are achieved with an emphasis on foliage,
where waterfalls of green provide the setting for a

Right: A number of elements are used in this
contemporary design: curves contrasted with the
perpendicular palm, rounded foliage, dark greens against
pale walls, and the pleasing effects of a pastel palette.

few, spotlighted hibiscus. Gardens with drier,
succulent landscapes need careful planning if the dry
plants are to coexist with moisture-loving hibiscus,
but it can be done. Hibiscus in containers, or
embedded semi-containers kept separate from the
succulents, can be treated separately, and moisture
retention can be aided by thick mulching.

Hibiscus flowers are not to be underrated. A
healthy, vigorous hibiscus – which is what they all
should be – proclaims its presence boldly. So
however you use them, give them the space and the
light they need and they, in their turn, will
illuminate your garden and your home.

Opposite: Hibiscus in small places: a narrow, paved
pathway, lushly planted on both sides, seems more like
a rainforest than a confined inner-city garden, an effect
easily created with container plants.

CHAPTER 6

# Pruning and Year-round
# Maintenance

## Pruning

Left unpruned, all hibiscus soon become shapeless and messy, and their flowers fewer, smaller and duller. Most hibiscus are evergreen. Apart from a cluster of species classified as herbaceous, which includes smaller annual or biennial sub-shrubs found growing in the wild, the only two fully deciduous species in cultivation are H. *syriacus* and H. *mutabilis*. These two hardy shrubs require heavy pruning to perform well, for like their tropical relations, they flower on new wood. Prune these two species only in winter, when the branches are bare. Other hibiscus should never be pruned in winter.

Early spring – at the start of the growing season – is the time to prune your tropical hibiscus. Occasionally, there may also be a need for a mid-season trim when the plant is in active growth, especially in warm climates. Most experienced growers prune just as cooler weather gives way to warm and when observation reveals the swelling of new growth buds. Don't wait for these buds to open out fully into leaves, but strike just before. Such timing will give you control over your plant by directing it where to put its energy. If you wait until after the new foliage has shot away, you've already lost some control, for the trimmings you discard are the wasteful product of the plant's energy reserves which might better have gone into leaves and blooms where you want them.

Opposite: A well-shaped and maintained shrub of 'Samoan Orange' in a street setting.

It is likely that along with the new foliage growth, you'll also be sacrificing flower buds. Don't think of this as a loss. Remember that you'll get far more flowers from pruning, because from each pruned branch or stem three new stems will grow in its place.

The purpose of pruning is to improve the shape of your hibiscus and to improve the vigor of its main branches (upright or spreading, depending on the hybrid) while also opening up the center to air circulation and sunlight, thereby encouraging new blooms. Pruning is more than just reducing the length of the branch and the number of its side shoots, for it also involves cleaning up any dead wood, removing weak or bug-eaten branches – and any diseased ones, of course – and cutting away any misshapen, spindly, odd-angled or aesthetically displeasing branches. Pruning means attaining desired shapes, and desired shapes can include espaliered and standard forms (see Chapter 5). If you prune wisely and your hibiscus are well-nourished, they will repay you with abundant and bountiful blooms.

By cutting back previous years' hardwood to reduce size, and by removing unwanted stems to induce vigor and shape, the result is likely to be a bush about two-thirds the pre-trimmed size. A healthy plant will tolerate even harder pruning to half size, or you may wish to take away only an eighth, or a quarter if the plant is young. With young shrubs, and sometimes even with larger ones, some experienced growers prefer to pinch out the first new

Cultivars of hardy *H. syriacus* , such as 'Flying Flag', need heavy pruning in spring.

growth rather than prune a longer branch, claiming that this method results in a thick-textured, better shape; they save the radical one-third-off prune for mature specimens.

Now for the actual cutting part. Make sure your secateurs and lopping shears are sharp and scrupulously clean, so that your cuts are likewise sharp and clean. Cut at a slight slant as with all hardwood, about a 45° angle, with the highest part of the slant just above a bud or "eye". This will allow water to run off rather than collect on the wound. A jagged cut will invite bacterial infection.

To remove unwanted stems growing at angles from the framework, cut at a fraction beyond the join. This applies also to those very low branches that sweep the ground near the base of the trunk. These branches are often never allowed to grow. While some gardeners like the appearance of bushiness right to the ground, others argue for their removal for reasons of hygiene, and say that space at ground level makes mulching and maintenance easier.

Opinion is also divided about the use of pruning tar. Sealing over the cut immediately following surgery is believed to prevent infection and promote health, but many arborists now eschew this practice with forest trees in favor of allowing the tree to self-seal its wound. Self-sealing occurs, they say, when the cut is made further out on the limb from where it joins the trunk, so that when this amputated stump naturally rots away, the wound left on the trunk is smooth.

Hibiscus growers will have to make up their own minds, but with ever-present threats of garden pests and diseases, they may feel some security in keeping on hand a cautionary tube of tar.

Neglected shrubs that have matured into quite hefty trees need a bold approach. First, feed and water them well over the growing season to promote health, then, after a winter rest period, arm yourself with a strong, well-sharpened pruning saw (and arm yourself with strong resolve, too), and lop down the entire tree to about table height, retaining half a dozen, at most, strong branches that open outwards, vase shaped, while removing inner-angled branches that clutter the center. Clean up completely the ground below. Now, with more than half your bush or tree gone, together with by far the greater portion of the foliage, resist the urge to feed it. There is insufficient foliage left to take up and release moisture, and adding nutrients, especially in concentrated form, can harm the bush, so leave it to recover. Recovery may take another whole season, but in time it will flourish fully. The foliage and flowering will both be invigorated.

At the other extreme, in the very small garden that is perhaps a mere extension of an apartment, pruning may need to be light but more frequent during the growing season to keep a small bush compact. The purpose-bred, tub-sized hybrids that are now available make it possible to fill a miniature garden with a number of continuously flowering hibiscus of modest dimensions, and they can be kept that size by pruning.

Pruning goes hand in hand with transplanting, planting out and potting, feeding, watering and mulching, so this is the time to consider a maintenance checklist for year-round hibiscus culture of both in-ground and container plants.

## Maintenance of tropical hibiscus

### At the start of spring
Prune. In cool climates, potted hibiscus that have overwintered under shelter can be brought out into the garden. All plants, whether in the ground or in pots, should be fed at this time.

### As the season advances
Apply a dressing of compost and, as temperatures start to rise, mulch. Mid-spring is a good time to relocate any plants and to plant out new ones. If pruning was earlier overlooked, it can be done now.

### At the start of summer
Regular watering may be necessary, depending on rainfall. There will be plenty of fresh foliage and the first full flush of flowers appearing (later in cooler climates). Weed. Watch for insects: whenever possible pick them off, squash them, or hose them completely away. Serious infestation may need more serious treatment.

### Mid-summer
Increased heat will bring increased pests, and spraying may be necessary. Mulch can be topped up. A light but frequently applied layer is better than a heavy infrequent one. Feed and water. This is likely to be the time of greatest demand for moisture. Occasional mid-summer pruning can be done, or may be necessary, on vigorous shrubs. This is the time for taking cuttings for propagating.

### Late summer to early fall
Keep watering and topping up mulch, tapering off as fall draws to a close. Check for general health, and watch in particular for insect infestation. Flowering should be at its best, and blooms longer-lasting. In cooler climates this will be the time of the last feed of the season.

### In late fall
Gather your last hibiscus blooms (along with your last tomatoes) and decorate your dining table. Only in warm areas should you continue to feed the plant. In cool climates prepare protective measures for ground-grown hibiscus, and move potted ones to shelter for the winter.

CHAPTER 7

# Pests, Diseases, and Solutions to Problems

Everyone knows the cliché, "the answer lies in the soil", and the claim that strong, healthy plants are disease-resistant, and the familiar refrain about "prevention being better than cure" … they are all true. All are applicable to hibiscus culture. So look to the soil, the siting, the moisture, the nutrients and the care, and ensure they are of top quality. Problems should then be minimal.

## The organic philosophy

The aim of all organic practices – permaculture, biodynamics, natural farming – is not just to reduce and ideally to eliminate the use of toxic chemicals that are harmful to humans, animals, plants and the planet, but to understand the processes of nature in order to participate, rather than to interfere.

This means a change in thinking. Instead of thinking monoculture on a massive scale, think biodiversity over a smaller area. Instead of thinking of insects as pests (remembering that pesticide manufacturers are powerful and influential), think of them as part of the natural order, with the plant-damaging insects kept in check by predators. Instead of thinking of perfection in ornamental and edible plants as blemish-free (sales conditioning), know that nature is not driven by glossy advertising. Think always of the way plants live without interference from humans.

Opposite: Plant health is evident in this residential garden where foliage and flowers are vigorous and buds numerous. ('Peggy Walton' is in the foreground.)

### Food for resistance

If you feed your hibiscus with compost – good-quality, balanced compost – you can never give them too much. Conversely, if you feed any plant with chemical fertilizers, you can easily give them too much. Too much can kill off all microlife. With edible plants, too much can contribute to cancer-promoting nitrites, and the imbalance that can result from overfeeding with artificial fertilizers can create pest and disease problems. Nitrogenous fertilizers in particular can be harmful because they promote rapid soft growth that attracts sucking insects.

Just as mammalian predators pick off the runt of the herd, so insects will overcome the weakest of the crop. If you doubt that compost is resistance food, try an experiment using both organic and inorganic fertilizers by growing carrots or cabbage in two lots. Give one lot the best compost you can and the other lot a nitrogenous fertilizer, such as sulfate of ammonia. The latter will quickly be eaten by pests.

Another analogy is stress: stress in humans results in vulnerability to colds, flu and infectious diseases. Stress in plants makes them similarly susceptible.

A soil rich in organic matter not only provides nutrients but inhibits the growth of fungal and bacterial diseases, such as *phytophthora*, by encouraging the natural antibiotic activities of mycorrhizal fungi. And of course, the texture of such a medium provides hibiscus roots with that high air-filled porosity they need. When they are healthy, well-fed hibiscus shrug off or outgrow pest damage.

## Stability in the garden

Aim to provide all plants with the conditions they need – if you can't, don't grow them. Aim for both lateral and vertical diversity, by matching plants with the conditions that suit them at every level, from ground-covering creepers through mid-high shrubs to the top of the canopy.

A stable garden does not contain impossibly difficult plants from quite different climates and conditions. Nor does it grow a huge number of similar plants in isolation from all others. And apart from the procedure of planting and transplanting, a stable garden is not routinely dug or hoed. Rather, layers are allowed to build up in the way a rainforest floor accumulates. Mulching and layering duplicate the processes of nature.

A stable garden in which natural pest control is practiced will always have a constant, but manageable, supply of pests providing food for a constant number of predators. Both are accepted as part of the ecosystem. Not all insects are bad – some are predators, some never cause plant damage, and others never build up their numbers.

## Companion planting for insect control

Companion planting is a component of the stable garden, but it is not a cure-all. On its own it is ineffectual: it doesn't rid the garden of pests, but it does aid diversity and stability. Through releasing different scents, through utilizing different levels of soil, and by occupying different garden spaces in certain combinations, companion planting can attract, or repel, specific insects. For example, plants which attract aphids and are good companions for hibiscus include the annuals feverfew, coriander and nasturtium, and *Hyssopus officinalis*.

# Hibiscus pests

Some hibiscus pests are worse than others. The larval grubs of garden butterflies can chomp their way through many a hibiscus leaf, but their harm is mostly visual. There are grubs which live off the foliage of shrubs and soft-wooded trees and other grubs which usually hatch out simultaneously. This means that if you find one, you'll find more. Watch closely for them, especially in the early morning, and if you discover them in the early stage, you may be able to pick off and destroy the whole batch.

## Chewing insects

Beetles too can be picked off. Apart from the flea-like bronze beetle (*Eucolaspis brunnea*), which leaps too quickly to be caught, most beetles can be hand removed if the bush is not first disturbed.

Snails and slugs, though voracious chewers, are a threat only to fresh new leaves, mainly on young plants. The best natural control is plentiful bird life. Other chewing pests include grasshoppers and katydids, those bright-green, well-camouflaged, flying bugs. Stick insects are also chewers, but fortunately don't often bother hibiscus. Excelling at camouflage on the bush, the females lay eggs which drop to the ground and emerge as nymphs in spring, climbing up the stem to feed on new leaves. A simple way to prevent them getting there is to band the base of the trunk or stem with a ring of grease – try Vaseline – that stops them in their tracks.

## Sucking insects

Sucking insects may be less conspicuous. Although the green vegetable bug, *Nezara viridula*, and its immature form with the colorful mosaic back are often easy to spot, most sucking insects are a lot smaller. Scales are only $1/16$th in (1 mm) long; spider mites, pinprick-sized pests, can cover the undersides of leaves; powdery or fluffy mealy bugs are a menace, and there's always the common aphid. Be alert for these. Evidence of their presence is white spot or chlorosis of the leaves (spider mites), misshapen buds (aphids), or sooty mould (by-product of mealy bugs and aphids).

To avoid spraying other than a last resort, try first squashing these pests by hand or removing them with

Pests of the tropics: while gardeners in cooler climates might be alarmed at these creatures, they belong in Queensland, Australia, where this picture was taken. The seedhead chewers do less visible damage than the leaf-eating grasshopper, which in turn is less of a menace than the Queensland hibiscus beetle.

a strong-pressured hose. Squashing or hose-blasting mealy bugs will probably not work though, because they coat themselves and the surrounding surface with a waxy substance that resists dislodgment. For mealy bugs, try a paintbrush application of water mixed half-and-half with methylated spirits. Spot applications of this sort (i.e. using a paintbrush) are always environmentally safer than wide-coverage spraying.

Thrips can be difficult to deter as they are fast movers. They are worst in dry conditions, and are not usually a problem in moist areas. Frequent hosing and misting can eliminate them. Whitefly infestation most often occurs in heated glasshouses. It shouldn't be a problem for the home garden where hibiscus have good air circulation.

Not yet present in the U.S.A., but a possible threat to horticulture, is the pink hibiscus mealy bug, *Maconellicoccus hirsutus* (green). It is typically observed as clusters of small, soft-bodied insects in cotton-like masses. Symptoms include twisted and distorted leaves and shoots, and unopened flowers which often shrivel and die. Be especially careful if importing any plant matter.

## Other pests

A big problem in Florida is gall midge. It lays its eggs in the flower buds, which the larvae then damage. The buds eventually drop, and this bud-drop is the most obvious sign of the pest. Any plants from Florida should be carefully checked.

To rid plants of this pest, remove all dropped buds or buds that begin to mold. Regularly apply orthene to the foliage and buds, and diazinon to the soil. (See "Chemical control", page 69.)

Another problem is Japanese beetle, *Popillia japonica*, fond of buds and flowers. Adult beetles can be controlled by spraying malathion, rotenone, sevin or methoxychlor.

There are other pests of course, most notably, perhaps, the dreaded hibiscus beetle (*Macroura concolor*) – scourge of hibiscus gardens in Queensland, Australia, to which it is fortunately confined.

## Natural controls and non-toxic pesticides

For most of the above-mentioned insects, natural controls should be tried. Among natural predators are hoverflies, which can consume huge numbers of aphids and also eat mites and scale insects; praying mantids, which are fully carnivorous and eat aphids, leaf hoppers, caterpillars, beetles and sometimes moths; spiders, which besides consuming flies feed on the larvae of moths and whiteflies; and, best of all, the ever-friendly ladybug. Ladybugs should be encouraged everywhere. Upon hatching, their larvae start immediately to eat aphids, mealy bugs, woolly aphids, thrips and other sap suckers, and they continue into adulthood to clean up these menaces.

Non-toxic sprays should be used with caution, not because of harm to humans but because indiscriminate use can kill both the targeted insect and its predators. The non-toxic preparations described here are short-lived and break down quickly, so they should be used up quickly. Pyrethrum (make your own from *Tanacetum cinerariifolium*, or buy the ready-made produce from garden centers) is a broad-spectrum insecticide. Garlic spray (soak 3 oz (85 g) of whole unpeeled garlic in mineral oil for 24 hours and add 1 pint (600 ml) of water in which a bar of soap has been dissolved; strain, dilute by five times, and spray) will work if it is eaten – it is not a contact spray – and can kill **stink bugs** and **the mosaic-backed vegetable bug**. Chile spray (1 cup of fresh chilli peppers pulped with $1/2$ cup of dried chilli and 1 cup of water) controls **caterpillars and loopers**, which are also deterred by sprinkled cayenne pepper. Buttermilk spray ($1/4$ cup of buttermilk and 2 cups of flour mixed with 1 gallon (5 liters) of water) will control **mites** when applied to the undersides of leaves every two days. Onion spray can be good for **scale**, **thrips**, **aphids** and **mites** (pour $3/4$ pint (500 ml) boiling water over $2^1/4$ lbs (1 kg) of chopped unpeeled onions and strain; dilute 20 times with water for spraying). Applications of ash from the fireplace, provided it is wood ash and dry, can control leaf-eating **earwigs**, **grasshoppers** and **katydids**. Some gardeners recommend diluted antiseptic solution as a good general insecticide.

While chemical insecticides which are systemic (such as Malathion or Maldison) can cause complete defoliation and are to be avoided, milder non-toxic systemics, such as neem oil, can be tried. This oil, widely used in India for a host of purposes, including keeping weevils from food stores, can be made from the leaves of the neem tree. As most

hibiscus growers are unlikely to have a neem tree at hand, you can buy the commercial oil and dilute it at a rate of one part oil to 200 parts (warm) water. The diluted solution does not store, so use it at once. it is safe to spray on sucking and plant-feeding pests because it doesn't harm the beneficial predators – or humans – and if applied early enough can suspend the egg-laying-to-larvae cycle of most insect pests.

Be careful with all the above mixtures. Although they use safe substances, they should be made up in special utensils kept separate from those used for food preparation, clearly labeled, and stored apart from kitchen ingredients.

You can also try traps. Cut a piece of white or yellow cardboard the size of your hand, and coat it with Vaseline. Nail it to a stake or tie to a hibiscus branch. Insect pests, especially night-flying ones, will be lured to it, as they are to all light, and will stick fast. Such a simple device is good for assessing what is in your local insect population. Try it and you'll be surprised at the sticky collection. A "trap" with a different purpose, that of catching **aphids**, can be made from a liquid containing sugar and yeast.

Another non-toxic suggestion is a diluted yeast-based spread laid around the garden in small quantities to attract predators such as hoverflies and lacewings, both of which feed on aphids.

An easily replicated recipe for "The Good Oil" from Hibiscus World in Queensland, Australia, uses equal-parts vegetable oil and liquid dishwashing detergent, diluted at the rate of 2 tsps (10 ml) to 4 cups (1 liter) of water. It is reportedly effective both at killing insects and repelling them.

Be aware that none of these sprays or strategies will completely eliminate your plant-damaging insects, but eradication should not be your objective. Aim instead to manage garden problems by keeping a balance of some pests and some predators. (If you did succeed in exterminating all the damaging insects which are the food of their predators, the natural balance would be upset, predators would keep away, and so the next infestation of pests would reach plague proportions.) 

On the subject of predators, feline predators add to pest problems by keeping birds out of gardens. Insectivorous birds actually consume huge numbers of pests if given the chance. It may be possible to train cats not to catch birds if disciplined from an early age, but really, all cats catch birds. A cat-free garden is often the most pest-free.

## Hibiscus diseases

*Phytophthora*, the soil-borne wilt disease associated with soils that dry out in summer and are wet in winter, can kill many ornamental shrubs, including hibiscus. It pays to avoid the kind of conditions favorable to *phytophthora* because affected plants usually do not recover. The problem rarely occurs where hibiscus are given good drainage and ample compost.

"Collar rot", visible as a browning discoloration, often slimy, at the root join, is prevalent where winters are cool and damp, and drainage poor. You can try a treatment of removing all affected stems and bark and painting the discolored area with Bordeaux paste. Clear the surrounding ground completely and spray with a strong garlic solution. **Sclerotina rot** affects stems at ground level. Repeated applications of strong garlic or chamomile tea can help.

If your hibiscus has succumbed to rot and you want to replant in the same spot – inadvisable but sometimes unavoidable – you must first improve the site. Start by removing the affected plant and burning it, then dig up the whole area beyond root depth and spread, distributing the infected soil in an unimportant area, such as plugging a hole in the driveway. Some gardeners advocate lighting a fire and spreading it over the entire site before refilling, as fire will kill off any remaining pathogens. The next step is to infill for drainage by lining the cavity with a layer of pumice mixed with fine gravel or pumice over coarser stones, adding sand, then filling the cavity with new topsoil. To be extra-cautious, use sterilized potting mix.

Besides diseases of the soil, there are fungal diseases that can affect foliage. **Leaf spot** is the main one to watch for. Contained plants may be slightly more susceptible to it than in-ground plants, especially when positioned in places with less air circulation. Dark brown or black spots on leaves indicate the presence of pathogens which are most active in wet weather. Heavily infected leaves, where the individual spots have merged to discolor the entire leaf, will result in shedding, and shrubs so depleted can probably only be salvaged by the application of a fungicidal spray, such as Bordeaux. Liquid Bordeaux can be bought from garden retailers or made at home to an exacting recipe of copper sulfate and calcium hydroxide. Bordeaux paste uses the same two ingredients less diluted, with skim-milk powder for viscosity.

In general, compost and mulch are the best root-rot preventatives. Dolomite sprinkled on the area can also help. An all-purpose spray for fungal prevention can be made from a "weak tea" of nettles, comfrey, yarrow or horseradish. Even better, a weak liquid poured off from seaweed soaked in fresh water has a four-fold benefit: it is a foliar fertilizer, it promotes frost-resistance, it is an insect repellent and a fungicide, and the residual seaweed can be composted or used as a mulch.

## Chemical control

Gardeners who choose to use toxins are strongly urged to use them only as a last resort – and sparingly. Never spray in sunlight or in the heat of day. Insecticides containing the chemical carbaryl and diazinon are considered effective, while fungicides containing triforine and copper oxy-chloride are also used in the nursery industry. Avoid benomyl as it is one of the most hazardous of all.)

Never combine insecticides with fungicides as the combination can be toxic to hibiscus as well as humans. Protective clothing and equipment use are your responsibility. The possibility or risk of any spray drift is likewise your responsibility, and in most municipalities this is now upheld by law.

---

## Eight rules of garden hygiene

· Monitor your plants
· Remove and burn diseased or infected leaves or plants
· Prune out dead wood
· Pick fallen or rotting fruit from fruit trees
· Keep out pollutants from neighbors, roads and traffic
· Do not use toxic pesticides, and use organic ones with discrimination
· Encourage birds
· Compost

---

## Solutions to other problems

### Sparse foliage

Apart from insect infestation or the general poor conditions that result from undernourishment, the most frequent cause of sparse foliage is insufficient sun. Site hibiscus in maximum sun.

### Crinkled leaves

Check for aphids or leaf hoppers on the undersides of leaves. Large colonies of aphids can suck the life out of leaves before they are noticed. Remove the affected leaves along with the offending insects. If the infestation is severe, try spraying.

### Deformed and sickly foliage

If it is possible or likely that your hibiscus has been exposed to systemic insecticides, it will quickly sicken. Hibiscus do not tolerate systemic chemicals,

such as maldison, which are absorbed by the plant. Good feeding and watering may help it recover.

### Yellow leaves

Yellowing of leaves at the base of branches and stems occurs naturally as the hibiscus sheds old foliage. If yellowing occurs higher up the stem, especially at the growing tips, it could indicate magnesium or iron deficiency – trace elements easily added to the soil. Alternatively, the discoloration could be a sign of over-watering or over-feeding with chemical fertilizers, in which case suspend both. Yellowing is another sign of exposure to systemic insecticides.

### Yellow leaves with green veins

Yellow leaves with green veins are a clear indication of iron deficiency. Apply a good feeding of compost and manure, and scratch in kelp meal or seaweed. Iron chelate is often recommended specifically to target the deficiency. Dig this in lightly – never pack down tightly around the stem. Mulch, kept clear from the base of the stem, can also help.

### Other leaf discoloration

Brown margins might be windburn, in which case watering and light feeding can restore health. Persistent and prolonged windburn, indicative of a windy climate to which hybrids may not be suited, is a problem that might be best solved by replacing hybrids with wind-tolerant coastal species, such as those described in Chapter 4.

Salt toxicity also shows up as brown leaf margins. Treat with generous watering. Leaves that turn brown at the tips, purple at the edges, and become brittle could indicate a lack of potassium.

### Frost damage

Once frost has damaged your hibiscus, there's nothing you can do. If severe, the plant may not recover at all; if light, it will struggle back of its own accord to produce new growth in spring. *Do not prune affected parts until the weather has warmed and new growth is established*. If you live where frosts can be expected every winter, you may consider pot culture to enable you to move the plant to shelter each year.

## Weeds

Any weeds growing around a hibiscus are competing with it for nutrients. Remove them. Remember that the feeding roots of hibiscus are very close to the surface, depending on the same top few inches of soil occupied by weeds. The easiest way to keep the area weed-free is to thoroughly clear it before covering with a layer of mulch; the mulch will keep the weeds at bay.

## Lawn encroachment

When hibiscus are sited in a lawn, an area of about 3 square feet (1 square meter) should be kept clear of competing growth. Mulching will deter the grass from encroaching again.

## Lichen

Gray, green or silver lichens occasionally establish themselves on old mature trees. They won't bother the hibiscus but may bother the gardener. (Some gardeners love and encourage lichens.) It would have to cover and smother the whole shrub before harming it. However, if you want to remove the growth, scrub it off with a scrubbing brush or apply Bordeaux paste in winter.

## Ants

Many ant species are valuable predators. They only invade hibiscus if there's something there for them to feed on, and although the odd ant may be attracted to nectar, ants in large numbers are usually after the honeydew excreted by aphids or mealy bugs. Deal with the aphids and the ants will go too. Moisture is an ant deterrent – they increase in dry places – as is pyrethrum spray. Banding the base of the hibiscus stem with Vaseline will prevent ants from traveling further up.

## Poor flowering

Few flowers in an otherwise healthy plant may result from too much shade, or, if sun is adequate, from excessive nitrogenous feeding which promotes leaf growth at the expense of flower production. Bud damage may also be a cause.

## Buds but no flowers

If your hibiscus are under attack from borers or beetles penetrating the buds before they open, the ground will show the evidence. The treatment of removing all buds, both from the bush (including the tips of branches) and from the ground below, and burning them, followed by insecticidal spraying, should reduce the problem, but may not eliminate it.

Bud drop can also result from lack of water during warm sunny weather; it is important not to let hibiscus dry out.

## Flowers appear late in the season

The most likely cause of late blooming is sun and temperature – not enough sun and not warm-enough temperatures.

## Blooms change color

The hybrids sold today are the result of years of intensive hybridizing, of crossing one with another, and often backcrossing again to achieve desirable attributes. As with many such "manmade" garden plants, dominant features of parent plants or earlier ancestry occasionally appear after they have been bred out. Sometimes hibiscus revert to colors of an earlier form; sometimes they'll revert from double to single, from ruffled to unruffled, or from overlapped or windmill single to plain single. This happens most often out of season, while true-to-type blooms can be expected in summer and fall. If the problem persists, you could consider asking your supplier to replace the plant with another whose performance matches the description.

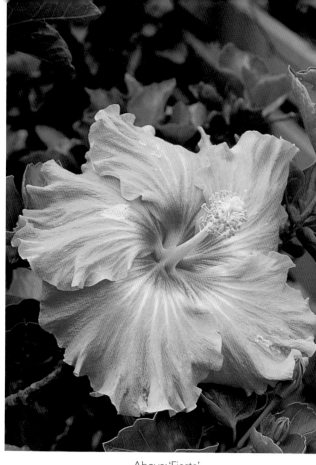

Above: 'Fire Engine'
Below: 'Lady Cilento'

Above: 'Fiesta'
Below: '442 Battalion'

Above: 'Sylvia Goodman'
Below: 'Ben Lexcen'

Above: 'Thora'
Below: 'June's Joy'

CHAPTER 8

# *Propagation*

Species hibiscus can be grown from seed and the offspring will be true to type. The species described earlier can be reliably propagated in this way (some of them self-seed prolifically), although the time from seed-sowing to a shapely bush in flower is a lot longer than the faster method of taking cuttings.

Hybrids, as distinct from species, cannot be propagated by seed to produce identical offspring. This is because the parental complexity of hybrids results in variable seed, with some seed reverting to one parent and others to an earlier ancestor, and so on, so it is possible for new progeny to resemble only slightly their seed-donor parents.

## Propagating species by seed

Germination may be hastened by scoring the surface of the seed with a razor blade, but the procedure is not essential. Use commercial starter mix in a shallow container. Press one or two seeds into the mix to about the same depth of the seed itself, and water well. Keep out of the sun at a temperature of 68°-77°F (20-25°C). Check that the mix stays moist but not wet. After about three weeks a new seedling, or two, will appear and shoots will develop. Once it has reached about 8 in (20 cm) high you can pot it, and flowering will be about another five to twelve months away, possibly longer.

## Other propagation methods

Other methods of propagation include grafting, air-

layering and tissue culture. These techniques call for some expertise, and most amateur gardeners would prefer to leave these to the specialists. Tissue culture, for example, the modern method of mass production, can only be done in laboratories. For most home gardeners who have admired the hibiscus of another gardener and want to acquire it, or whose own hibiscus is so pleasing they want more, or who are moving homes and can't take a large shrub with them, fortunately there's a simple method of reproduction: taking cuttings.

## Taking cuttings

In late winter or early spring, just before the shrub begins its first warmer-weather flush, select a hardwood stem for cutting. Nurserymen intent on production yields may take cuttings of softwood tips, particularly if parental material is in short supply, or medium wood, or hardwood, or all three of these, but the home gardener will find hardwood cuttings easiest to handle. Select the best stem you can find: straight, smooth, as thick as a pencil or thicker, and unblemished.

Now, using scrupulously clean secateurs, cut immediately below the node (i.e. where leaves or buds join the stem) at an angle of about 45°, and then trim to about 5-6 in (12-15 cm) long; professionals use a sharp knife for this task. Remove any leaves. Place the cuttings in a pot of coarse material, such as sand, perlite, or a mix of these, and include a little peat – about one part sand to one part peat. Don't push the stems deep into the medium – 1 in (3 cm) is plenty. Bottom heat is not

'Patricia Noble'

necessary, nor is rooting hormone powder. (Experiments have shown that the difference between applying hormone preparation and not, is about 20 percent; commercial growers aim for a 100 percent strike, but most home gardeners are probably happy with 60-70 percent.)

Place a hoop of wire over the pot by pushing each end of the wire down the side, to create a support for the plastic covering you should then attach. Position the pot in a warm spot away from direct sun. Warmth is important, even if bottom heat isn't (of course, commercial propagators always use bottom heat), so if the climate is cool, wait until the weather heats up or take it indoors. If the medium was well-watered at the start, further watering shouldn't be necessary, so you can forget all about the cutting and go forth into the garden. If you forget for long enough, you'll be agreeably surprised at seeing your cuttings when they've struck. This will take about 6 to 8 weeks if an optimum temperature of 68°-77°F (20° to 25° C) is main-

tained, and longer in cooler temperatures. Let them develop more green growth (another month or so), and when they start to really shoot away, put each one into its own individual pot. Should the strike be so successful and vigorous that the cuttings' fine roots are enmeshed, separate them gently by immersing first in clean water. Pot into a mix with some nutrition in it, using such ingredients as compost, peat, commercially bagged all-purpose potting mix, or quality loam with well-rotted manure – together with a generous scoop or two of coarse sand for drainage – and water well.

It is in these individual pots that your new hibiscus shrubs will start to develop. Keep them out of direct sun and watch over them until you feel they've grown enough to be ready to plant in the garden, or into the larger containers if you intend to keep them in. Before their final move outside, expose them gradually to more and stronger sunshine over a period of several weeks. Remember that slugs and snails are never interested in mature leaves – they much prefer the tasty new leaves of an infant plant, so be vigilant and you'll be rewarded.

Opposite top: 'Flower Girl'

Bottom: 'Molly Cummings'

# CHAPTER 9

# *Tropical Hibiscus in Cold Climates*

Everyone loves flowering plants and every gardener, sooner or later, takes up the challenge to grow them in areas beyond their comfort zone. This works both ways, hot and cold. But it is easier to succeed in growing a warm climate plant, such as hibiscus, in areas with cold winters where homes are heated, than for a gardener in the tropics to succeed with tulips or alpine bulbs. (Though they never give up! Even tulips have been known to bloom in warm regions through the use of refrigerators and by burying bulbs three times deeper than normal.)

In Canada and the northern states of the U.S.A., where winters are severe, growers have perfected a method of growing tropical hibiscus by bringing their potted plants indoors over winter.

Quebec, at a latitude of 47° north of the equator, is an example, where hibiscus are among the most popular garden plants grown in summer, while for six or seven winter months they grow indoors. Quebec's hibiscus have thrived. Indeed, much of the information which follows comes from the experience of growers in this city. (See also Chapter 3 on container culture.)

Container plants grown this way stay smaller for longer than they would in the tropics, where, left to their own devices, they can turn into trees. The advantage of a more moderate growth rate is

Opposite: Hibiscus make attractive container plants and grouped in varying heights, including here a standard, they create a showy display. Above right: A beautiful combination of plant and container.

portability. Container lifting can be tiring. So it is fortunate that hibiscus can be grown in fairly small containers relative to their size. A young, newly-acquired hibiscus does not need a large container, at least not until its roots become container-bound. To start with, a 10 in (25 cm) pot is ample.

## Potting mix

Both pot and mix must allow for fast drainage. This is imperative. A suggested mix to try is one part

Hibiscus grown in containers can be moved outdoors in warmer weather.

commercial potting mix (composed of peat moss, perlite and vermiculite) and one part compost, either commercially bagged or homemade. One brand of compost widely available in Canada and which has produced impressive results, contains marine organisms. Decomposed shrimp and seaweed are among the ingredients. (It is tempting to speculate that because hibiscus species are indigenous to coastal areas in the tropics and sub-tropics, they delight in marine-based compost.) Compost usually also contains bark and manure products which provide friability, assist drainage and supply nutrients.

The potting mix and the compost should be combined well, pressed but not packed hard, and should fill the container to about 1 in (2¹/₂ cm) below the rim.

## Watering
Summer watering outdoors will include rainfall, which benefits the plant more than faucet water, and as long as drainage is good, plants are unlikely to suffer from over-watering, particularly as this is a time of active growth and greater uptake.

But indoors is a different story. Fatalities occur too often through too frequent watering, which keeps the surface of the mix perpetually damp.

The growth of plants at this time is slow, meaning plants are unable to take up much moisture, making it easier for rot to set in. So care is needed. Use your fingers to check the surface soil. If the surface is damp, allow it to dry out before the next watering. Don't let it become sodden. The rule is: water less in winter and more during times of active growth.

## Fertilizing
Granular all-purpose fertilizers can be used when repotting or at the start of spring or summer, otherwise the recommended method is frequent applications of diluted liquid fertilizer, such as commercial products high in potassium and micro-nutrients. These usually come in powder form and are mixed with water, so you can control the strength. Diluted liquid fertilizer can be applied as frequently as every ten days in summer – but less indoors in winter. Obviously a very young small hibiscus needs less fertilizing than a larger bush.

## Pests
While hibiscus rarely succumb to disease, indoors pests can be a problem. Among them aphids, mealy bug, white fly and spider mites are most likely to cause damage.

With the worldwide trend away from using toxic chemicals in favor of organic methods, the recommended treatment is a soap-based insect-icide that can be used as a preventative as well as a cure.

Try commercial brands, or make your own by mixing 1¹/₂ teaspoons (7 ml) of dishwashing soap (with no phosphates) and one pinch of baking soda in 2 pints (1 liter) of water. Be sure to apply it to the undersides of leaves rather than the surface. Where aphids or spider mites are visible you can rub them dead with your fingers; if you can apply the liquid and snub out any insects at the same time, so much the better, as reinfestation will be less likely.

(One grower defeated mealy bugs, that annoyingly

Ideal container plants, these dwarf, purpose-bred hibiscus flower best in good light.

adhere to leaves with a waxy substance, by vaporizing pure alcohol – chemist's rubbing alcohol – and spraying it on the mealy bugs. The leaves remained unaffected. This was a one-off experiment, so imitators should proceed with caution!)

## Light

Light is crucial to the growth of tropical hibiscus in high latitudes. It plays a much greater role here than in the tropics and sub-tropics, where daylight hours vary less between summer and winter. In places like Montreal and New York the winter light is much shorter and measurably darker, and hibiscus kept indoors respond accordingly. While not exactly dormant, their growth is slowed. Conversely in summer, because daylight hours are so very much longer, it seems that the surfeit of light is too much for them, which is why they do better in half sun/half shade.

Indoors in winter it is important to provide the best light possible. A conservatory or bay window is ideal, otherwise give them a window on the south side – the larger the glass area the better.

The plants' receptors are finely tuned to the increase in daylight after the shortest day and by February they know that spring is approaching. The lengthening days trigger a growth spurt which becomes more apparent in March and April.

## Pruning

The purpose of all this care and nurture is to produce flowers and pruning is intended to assist, not thwart, bud production. For this reason pruning should be done in February just as growth is starting to respond to the lengthening light, so that by spring or early summer, when your hibiscus are established outdoors, blooming will begin. If pruning is delayed, flowering is delayed. Early pruning results in cheerful garden color at the time it is most wanted.

Prune stems at an angle using sterile tools (see Chapter 6) to cut away about one-quarter to one-third of the branch just above the node. Unless your plant is large and robust, and bigger than you can conveniently accommodate, such pruning may be all that's needed. On the other hand, new plants in the first few years may need no pruning at all.

Some gardeners give their plants an additional lighter prune in fall at the time of bringing them indoors, but this is not vital to plant health.

## Humidity

Humidity is not the same as watering. Moisture for uptake by the roots is essential for all plants, while their requirements for moisture in the air varies vastly from xerophytic cacti to rainforest species, just as the humidity present in the air varies from place to place – and from house to house. Many homeowners have electric humidifiers to keep the moisture content in the air at a comfortable level.

Humidifiers benefit tropical hibiscus. One of the advantages of positioning hibiscus close to windows is that they can absorb small amounts of condensation from the glass. If you don't have a humidifier and the air inside your home is dry, try spraying your plants with water mist. Another effective way of increasing humidity is to fill the saucer under the container with pebbles and place the pot on top of the watered pebbles where moisture will evaporate around the plant and can be replaced from time to time.

## Repotting

Repotting becomes necessary only when a plant has outgrown its container and the roots are tight and spiraled or container-bound. Spring is the time to repot. After freeing the plant you will need to gently untangle the roots and improve their shape. You can lightly prune both foliage and the root ends as much as seems necessary for the new container. Gentle handling of a healthy plant should not harm it.

Repot to a larger container. Remember that width is more important than depth and a wide container filled to about $1\frac{1}{2}$ in (4 cm) below the rim allows for a thin layer of mulch on top of the mix.

## Mulching

Mulch aids plant health. It can be bark, pine needles and small cones, wood-shavings or the excellent product that combines all these shredded together: cedar mulch. Mulching benefits the plant in several ways: it acts as insulation from temperature changes, protects surface roots from accidental damage, conserves moisture so that the need for watering is reduced and slowly breaks down to provide textural and nutritional matter. Hence flowering is increased.

## A year's indoor-outdoor cycle

After the February prune, new growth will appear through March and April. In early May if you live where spring starts early, or mid- to late May where winter lingers longer, you can introduce your indoor hibiscus to outside conditions. "Introduce" is the operative word, meaning a gradual process rather than a sudden uplifting into the full blast of bright light, which can cause shock. And any shock, any stress, will result in a weaker plant and fewer blooms. So do it gradually. Start with just one hour outside for the first day, then two hours the next, then three and so on – it could be nine to ten days or longer before your hibiscus are fully established in their summer position. Even then, an intermediate

These tropical hybrids are grown outdoors in pots in the ground during the summer months.

stage, such as against a wall with overhanging shelter for a week or two, can reduce the risk of shock.

In high latitudes the positioning of hibiscus outdoors in summer needs care. Experience has shown that they do not like a whole thirteen or fourteen hours of sun a day (perhaps because they originated in places with shorter daylight) and should therefore be sited where they will receive half shade. Morning sun and afternoon shade is ideal. So is a location under a lacy canopy of leaves receiving dappled sunlight. But all-day sun should be avoided.

This is a good time for renewing the top inch with fresh all-purpose potting mix and applying a few granules of fertilizer.

Gardeners with confined outdoor areas usually arrange their container plants with the container itself fully exposed; others with larger gardens may prefer to bury their pots in the ground. Care should be taken to ensure buried containers have good drainage in the soil and subsoil all around, as waterlogging can be fatal. There is a third way, a compromise between a free-standing container and a buried one, whereby the bottom half of the pot only is buried, leaving the top half exposed. Bark mulch is then loosely mounded in a gentle slope all around the outside of the container and lightly over the surface, so that it is no longer visible.

Once your hibiscus are established in summer mode, water regularly and liquid fertilize at intervals of every two weeks or so, if the solution is diluted and

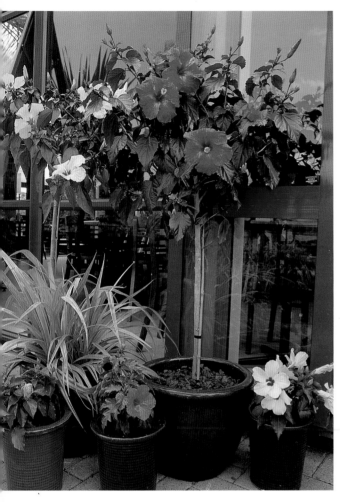

Grown in pots, hibiscus are very portable, easily taken indoors when cold temperatures hit.

tenance, such as preventative spraying with soap solution, can be done. Either spread newspapers to protect furnishings or take the plants to the bathtub and work on them there.

Plant growth will slow down during December and January at the time of the shortest days. This is when your plants need as much light as possible, as well as good air circulation, though strong drafts should be avoided. Avoid positioning plants near sources of heat or where there are extremes of temperature change.

Be careful not to over-water at this time and be alert for pests or diseases. In February it will be time to prune and look forward to the next season's growth.

Among those tropical hybrids recommended for their reliability in indoor-outdoor culture are:
FIFTH DIMENSION (Multi-colored: red eye, white veins, gray and orange.)
HIGH VOLTAGE (Single, dark carmine center shading to rose pink.)
DRAGON'S BREATH (syn 'Roy Kautz'. Single, ruffled rose-red with deeper center.)
PRIMA BALLERINA (Double flower, ruffled buff cream with red center.)
JAMI-LOU (Single, ruffled cerise-pink with gold eye.)
TAMIBON (Large blooms, twisted overlap petals in pale canary yellow and lavender.)
THE PATH (Single flower, multi-colored in pink and yellow.)

the plant large; less for smaller plants. Keep an eye out for pests and admire the blooms.

At the onset of fall, in mid- or late September, or possibly later in milder districts, prepare to bring your hibiscus indoors. Check for damage and insects, tidy up spent blooms and dead stems and clip any exposed roots. You can also give your plants a light prune if you wish. Again, you can make use of shelters as a half-way stage, but this is not necessary and the hibiscus can go straight to their winter positions.

During the next six months or so any main-

# Lists of Hibiscus Hybrids

## Tropical hibiscus

The following tropical hybrids (of *H. rosa-sinensis* origin) are a selection from the thousands that are grown and sold around the world. It is impossible to name them all, and simultaneous or parallel hybridizing in different countries has sometimes resulted in the same plant having different names. This doubling-up is becoming more apparent today because of the increase in import-export mobility, as plant material from which to propagate, as well as live seedlings, are now transported by the thousand around the globe. While the name confusion is a disadvantage, the big advantage for the home gardener is that this increase in trade is enlarging the range of plants available for sale.

The following list is a selection from among the most popular named hybrids. While it makes no claim to be comprehensive, the list is likely to include many that are widely available.

As for descriptions of these hybrids, the details here are brief. (See also classifying descriptions in Chapter 2, Cultivation.) Bush classification refers to height only: low – up to 3 ft/1 m; medium – about 3 ft/1 m to over 6 ft/2 m; tall – over 7 ft/2.2 m and does not take into account shape, spread, or growth habit. Nor do they describe flower details, such as tufted or overlapping windmill petals, or consider which hybrids grow on their own roots and which can only be grown as grafted plants, and so on. The list should therefore be consulted in conjunction with nursery catalogs that usually provide fuller details, or, better still, with knowledgeable staff. Everywhere, the best source of reliable plants, and of advice in choosing them, is a local supplier.

In this list, the term "half-hardy" (HH) refers to tropical hybrids that have proved hardier than others as in-ground plants. These, in turn, are used as rootstock for more tender hybrids. Ask at your nursery for information about grafted plants.

Those hybrids followed by (C) are especially good container plants, in that they are slower-growing and smaller-flowered. However, all the hybrids named are suitable for containers.

| | |
|---|---|
| ALII UI (C) | single small tomato-red splashed with pale yellow, medium bush, good container plant |
| ALOHA | single cerise-pink with wide lemon-gold edge, medium bush |
| AMBER SUZANNE | double pink and white long-lasting blooms, medium bush |
| ANNIE WOOD | single cream and yellow with red eye, medium bush |
| APACHE | single orange with red eye, medium bush |
| BEACH BALL | double gold long-lasting blooms, medium bush |
| BEN LEXCEN | single apricot with pink eye, medium bush |
| BERRIED TREASURE | single lavender long-lasting blooms, tall bush |

| | |
|---|---|
| BIG APPLE | semi-double deep red, medium bush, prolific |
| BIG TANGO | single tomato-red with paler eye, low bush |
| BLACK KNIGHT | single dark red with cream spots and splashes, medium bush |
| BLACK MAGIC | single deep rose with black eye, long-lasting blooms, medium bush |
| BLAZEAWAY | single red, edged with orange, medium bush |
| BLUEBERRY TART | single lavender miniature flowers, weak spindly growth, but the color makes it a worthwhile addition to a collection |
| BRUCEII | single yellow with white eye, tall bush, vigorous and prolific |
| BUMBLE BEE | double orange and red, medium bush |
| CARNATION | double dark red, small picot-edged flower, low bush |
| CARNIVAL QUEEN | single ruffled, red with cream splashes, medium bush |
| CERES | double gold, small flower, medium bush |
| CHARCOAL (C) | single small brilliant-red, edged with brown, medium bush, good container plant |
| CHESTER FROWE | single orange-red, medium bush |
| CLOUD DANCER | semi-double, deep rose-pink, medium bush |
| COCONUT ICE | single pink with white spots, medium bush, must be grafted |
| COLOMBUS | single apricot, medium bush, shiny foliage, prolific |
| COPENHAGEN (C) | single orange-red, medium bush, good container plant |
| CORONA (C) | single small orange flower edged with yellow, with purple eye, medium bush, good container plant |
| CREOLE FLAME (C) | semi-double small brown flower, low bush, good container plant |
| CRIMSON BAY (C) | single bright yellow with carmine-red eye, medium bush, good container plant |
| CROWN OF BOHEMIA (C) | double gold, medium bush, hardy, good container plant |
| CUBAN VARIETY | single apricot with red eye and veining, medium-tall bush, prolific |
| CULTURED PEARL | semi-double pink, tall bush |
| DADDY'S GIRL | single lavender, medium bush |
| DOROTHY | single cream with red eye, low bush (syn MADONNA, RITA) |
| DOUBLE DATE (C) | Double pink, medium bush, good container plant |
| DUSKY BEAU | single ruffled silvery lavender with plum eye, medium bush |
| EL CAPITOLIO | single fluted bright scarlet miniature flower, low bush |
| ESTRELLA RED (C) | single velvet-red, almost black, large flower, medium bush, good container plant |
| EURILLA SUNSHINE | single yellow with red eye, tall bush |
| FANTASIA PINK | single satiny pink small flower, tall bush, prolific |
| FANTASIA WHITE | single white small flower, tall bush, prolific |
| FIFTH DIMENSION | multi-colored; red eye, white veins, beige to orange edge, gun-metal gray, medium bush |
| FIJI ISLAND | single deep pink with darker eye, small flower, tall bush, vigorous |
| FIRE ENGINE | single bright orange-red, medium bush |
| FLAMINGO STAR | double pink, large flower, medium bush |
| FLORIDA SUNSET | single orange with red eye, small flower, tall bush |

| | |
|---|---|
| FOR PETE'S SAKE | single lavender with red eye, medium bush |
| FLYING DUTCHMAN | single apricot-orange with white eye, medium bush |
| FOSTER BRADY | semi-double pink and cream with red eye, tall bush |
| 442 BATTALION | single khaki with pale mauve eye, upright medium bush, prolific |
| FRANK'S LADY | single pink with gold edge and white veins, medium bush |
| FREDDIE BRUBAKER | single gold with red eye, large crepe bloom, low bush, prolific |
| FULL MOON | double yellow, tall bush, prolific |
| FUTURAMA | double apricot and lavender, medium bush |
| GENERAL CORTEGES (HH) | single scarlet red, tall bush, attractive foliage, half-hardy |
| GLORIA | single orange, small flower, tall bush |
| GOLD | single bright yellow-gold, crepe flower, low bush, glossy foliage |
| GOLD DUST | single golden apricot with cream splashes, ruffled, medium bush |
| GOLD COAST CITY | double orange large flower, medium bush |
| GOLDEN BELLE (C) | single yellow large flower, low bush, good container plant |
| GOLDEN PLATTER | single gold with pale pink eye and white halo, low bush |
| GRANNY'S BONNET | double lavender multi-colored large blooms, low bush |
| GREAT SATAN | single apricot-brown with yellow splashes and red eye, low bush |
| GREAT WHITE | single large creamy white, tall bush |
| GWEN MARY | single pink, medium bush |
| HARVEST MOON | semi-double yellow large flower, medium bush |
| HAWAIIAN RED | single deep red, ruffled, medium bush |
| HERM GELLER | single honey-brown and gold with red eye, medium bush |
| HONEY DO | single gold large flower, medium bush |
| HOT SHOT | single red and yellow, ruffled, medium bush |
| HUMMINGBIRD | single pink with red veins, small flower, low bush |
| ICELAND GIRL | semi-double white with red eye, medium bush |
| INDIAN MAID | single orange with creamy yellow patches, medium bush |
| INSIGNUS | single gold with red eye and white halo, medium bush |
| ISABELLE BARLING | single lavender-pink and deep pink veins, medium bush, prolific |
| ISLAND EMPRESS | double cerise-pink with burgundy center, tall bush |
| ISOBEL BEARD | semi-double lavender with red eye, medium bush, prolific |
| JALMA | single pink with red eye, medium bush |
| JAYELLA | single gold and tan large flower with red eye, tall bush |
| JERRY SMITH | double rich yellow, low bush |
| JOL WRIGHT | double orange large flower, low bush |
| KATY D | semi-double rose-pink, medium bush |
| KENMER RHAPSODY | semi-double salmon large flower, tall bush |
| KYLIE RITCHIE | single orange with yellow edge, medium bush |
| LADY CILENTO | single bright orange with yellow spots and stripes, tall bush |
| LAMBERTII (C) | double red, low bush, good container plant |
| LAVENDER LADY | single lavender with red eye, medium bush, prolific |
| LEMON CHIFFON | single lemon-yellow flushed pink with white eye, medium bush |

| | |
|---|---|
| LITTLE YELLA | single yellow, small flower, tall bush |
| LUTINO | single yellow with white veins and red eye, tall bush |
| MADONNA (C) | single creamy white with deep-red eye, low bush (syn DOROTHY, RITA) |
| MARJ DOLLISSON | single pink and cream with scarlet eye, large flower, low bush |
| MARJORIE CORAL (C) | single rose-pink with red eye large flower, medium bush |
| MAROON STARS | single red with yellow-cream blotches and purple eye, tall bush |
| MARY WALLACE (C) | single deep orange with yellow edges, medium bush |
| MELLIE MAY | single apricot and gold, tall bush |
| METEOR | single bright yellow with red eye and white veins, low bush |
| MINI SKIRT | single cerise-red with white spots and streaks, ruffled, low bush |
| MISS HAWAII (C) | semi-double orange, medium bush, slow-growing, good in containers |
| MISS LIBERTY | single cream with pink veins, medium bush |
| MISS NORTH MIAMI | single red, medium bush |
| MOLLY CUMMINGS (HH) | single rich velvety red, medium bush, half-hardy, reliable and easy |
| MONIQUE MARIA | double pink with apricot edge, ruffled, medium bush |
| MORNING STAR | single lavender-pink, medium bush |
| MOUNT SHASTA | double creamy white, ruffled, medium bush, glossy foliage |
| MRS HAYWOOD | single rich red, ruffled, medium bush |
| MYSTIC CHARM | single cerise-red with white border, low bush |
| MYSTIC HUE | single lavender-mauve, small flower, tall bush |
| NORMAN LEE (C) | single deep cerise with broad yellow edge, low bush, good container plant |
| ORANGE GROVE | single orange with red eye and pink halo, ruffled, tall bush |
| ORANGE MAGIC | single dark orange with apricot edges, medium bush |
| PA WALLACE | double red small flower, medium bush |
| PACIFIC PEARL | single lilac with red eye and silvery pink sheen, medium bush |
| PEEPING TOM | single red with orange border, medium bush |
| PINK CAMEO | single pink with purple eye, tall bush, vigorous |
| PINK DAWN | semi-double lavender-pink with paler edges, medium bush |
| PINK GEM | single pink with red eye, small flower, tall bush |
| PINK PSYCHE | single satin pink, small fringed flowers, tall bush |
| PINK RADIANCE | single deep pink with paler edges, medium bush, prolific |
| PINK RAYS | single pink and lemon with pink veins, medium bush |
| PINK SATIN | single pink, medium bush |
| PRECIOUS NOVA | single orange with gold edge, medium bush |
| PRIMROSE | single lemon with white eye, medium bush |
| PRO LEGATO | double deep purplish red, low bush |
| PSYCHE (HH) | single shiny red small flower, tall bush, half-hardy and prolific |
| PURPLE PASSION | single purple-red with burgundy eye and cream border, low bush |
| RASPBERRY CREPE | single pink crepe flower, medium bush |
| RED BOMB | single red with yellow spots, ruffled, medium bush |
| ROSE SCOTT (HH) | single rose-pink with red eye, tall bush, half-hardy, good as hedge |
| ROSS ESTEY | single pink and peach, ruffled, medium bush, prolific |

'Freddie Brubaker'

| RUBY ROSE | single pink with maroon eye, small flower, low bush |
| SABRINA | double cerise-red, ruffled, tall bush |
| SHARON DEE | single mauve with scarlet eye, tall bush |
| SHIRLEY HOWIE | single pink with cream borders, medium bush |
| SHOW BUSINESS | single pinkish red with yellow, medium bush |
| SHOW GIRL | double red, tall bush |
| SIBLING X | single red with white splashes, medium bush |
| SILVER ROSE | single lavender-pink with silvery eye, crepe flower, medium bush |
| SLEEPING SINGLE | single red with gold border, ruffled, medium bush |
| SNOW QUEEN | single red small flower, tall bush, striking white variegated leaves |
| SPRING SONG | single orange with pink eye, medium bush, fast growing |
| SPRINKLE RAIN | single salmon-pink with cerise eye, small flower, tall bush, prolific |
| STORMY DAYS (C) | double deep lavender fading to silver, medium bush, good container plant |
| SUMMER FLASH | single gold-orange, medium bush |
| SUNDOWN | single deep orange with yellow edges, low bush, prolific |
| SURFRIDER (C) | single orange with red eye, large flower, low bush, good container plant |

| | |
|---|---|
| SWEET AMBER | semi-double cream with red eye, low bush |
| TAMMY FAYE | single lavender-pink with red eye and apricot edges, medium bush |
| TANGO | single orange, medium bush |
| TEN THIRTY SEVEN | single orange and red, large flower, tall bush |
| THE PATH (C) | single pink-yellow multi-colored, low bush, good container plant |
| THE PEARL | single white-tinged pale pink, ruffled, medium bush |
| THORA | single cream and cerise-pink, small flower, tall bush |
| TOPSY | single gold and red, low bush, prolific, good beginner's hybrid |
| VASCO | single bright lemon with white eye, medium bush |
| VITAMIN C | semi-double pale yellow-gold, medium bush |
| VIVIENNE | single deep red, tall bush |
| VULCAN (C) | single velvet-red with pink eye, medium bush, good container plant |
| WHIRLS-N-TWIRLS | single yellow, medium bush |
| WHITE KALAKAUA | double white suffused with pale pink, tall bush (syn ELEPHANT EAR, PEARL HARBOR, BUTTERFLY WINGS) |
| WILMAE | single orange-brown with mauve eye, medium bush |
| YELLOW FIRE (C) | single yellow-gold, low bush, good in containers |
| YVONNE | single pale apricot with pink eye, tall bush, can be grown from seed |
| YO-YO | single orange with yellow eye, medium bush |
| ZELLIE WAEGNER | semi-double lemon and orange with deep red eye, medium bush |

## Selected hardy hybrids

Of the three hardy species two have been hybridized. The two hybridized species are *Hibiscus syriacus* (see page 32) and *H. moscheutos* (see page 35). New hardy hybrids are coming onto the market all the time, so check catalogs and garden centers for the latest releases.

### H. syriacus hybrids (Rose of Sharon, Althea)
*These hybrids grow between 4 and 6 ft (1.2 and 1.8 m), unless stated otherwise*

| | |
|---|---|
| ADMIRAL DEWEY | double pure white flowers |
| ALBA PLENA | semi-double pure white flowers |
| ANEMONIFLORA | (syn PAEONIFLORA) semi-double red with dark-crimson eye |
| APHRODITE | single large rose-red with large dark eye |
| ARDENS | semi-double lavender-mauve flowers |
| BLUE BIRD | (syn OISEAU BLEU) single large rich gentian-blue with purple center |
| BLUSHING BRIDE | double pink |
| BOULE DE FEU | double small purple-red flowers, low bush |
| CARNATION BOY | double lavender flowers |
| COELESTIS | single violet flowers streaked with white |
| COLLIE MULLENS | double light purple with magenta eye |
| DIANA | single large pure white flowers |

| | |
|---|---|
| DOUBLE WINE | double wine-red flowers |
| FLYING FLAG | single white with red flowers |
| HAMABO | single pink with reddish margins |
| HEIDI | violet-blue, low bush |
| HELENE | single white with dark-red eye and veins |
| HINO MARU | single pure white flowers |
| LADY STANLEY | semi-double soft pink flowers |
| LUCY | double magenta with dark-red eye |
| MIMIHARA | semi-double cream and crimson flowers |
| MINERVA | single large lavender flower with reddish-purple eye and veins |
| PURPUREUS VARIEGATUS | double maroon-red flowers that never quite open, variegated foliage |
| PURPUREA | semi-double purple with red eye and veins |
| RED HEART | single white flowers with red veins and center |
| ROSALINDA | semi-double purple flowers |
| RUBER PLENUS | double maroon-red flowers |
| SNOWDRIFT | semi-double white flowers |
| WHITE SUPREME | semi-double white flowers |
| WILLIAM SMITH | single pure white flowers |
| WOODBRIDGE | single wine-red flowers with red eye |

## H. *moscheutos* hybrids (Mallow, Rose Mallow, Swamp Hibiscus)
*All are singles and grow between 4 and 6 ft (1.2 and 1.8 m), unless stated otherwise*

| | |
|---|---|
| ANNE ARUNDEL | rosy-pink with red eye, from cuttings |
| BLUE RIVER | pure white, from cuttings |
| GEORGE RIEGEL | pink with red eye, from cuttings |
| DISCO BELLE | various shades of reds, pinks and white, from seed |
| DIXIE BELLE | various shades of reds, pinks and white, low bush, from seed |
| FRISBEE | various shades of reds, pinks and white, low bush, from seed |
| LADY BALTIMORE | bright rosy-pink with deep-red center, low bush, from cuttings |
| LORD BALTIMORE | deep-red, from cuttings |
| MALLOW MARVELS | various shades of reds, pinks and white, from seed |
| OLD YELLA | yellow with red eye, low bush, from cuttings |
| RIO CARNIVAL | various shades of reds, pinks and white, low bush, from seed |
| SOUTHERN BELLE | various shades of reds, pinks and white, from seed |
| SWEET CAROLINE | soft pink with deep-red eye, from cuttings |
| TEXAS GIANT HIBISCUS | (syn MUY GRANDE HYBRID) rose-pink, from cuttings |
| TURN OF THE CENTURY | two-toned white and pale pink, tall bush, from cuttings |

# Lists of Selected Tropical Hybrids for Particular Purposes

## Reliable beginner's plants
'Annie Wood'
'Molly Cummings'
'Ross Estey'
'Topsy'

## Suitable for containers
'Alii Ui'
'Charcoal'
'Copenhagen'
'Creole Flame'
'Crimson Bay'
'Crown of Bohemia'
'Double Date'
'Estrella Red'
'Golden Belle'
'Madonna' (syn 'Dorothy', 'Rita')
'Marjorie Coral'
'Mary Wallace'
'Miss Hawaii'
'Norman Lee'
'Stormy Days'
'Surfrider'
'The Path'
'Yellow Fire'

## Tolerant of cooler conditions (infrequent light frosts)
*Some of these are used as rootstock for less hardy hybrids*
'General Corteges'
'Molly Cummings'
'Psyche'
'Ross Scott'

## Low-growing
*Suitable for smaller gardens and patios*
'Big Tango'
'Carnation'
'Creole Flame'
'El Capitolio'
'Freddie Brubaker'
'Golden Belle'
'Granny's Bonnet'
'Hummingbird'
'Jerry Smith'
'Jol Wright'
'Madonna' (syn 'Dorothy', 'Rita')
'Marj Dollisson'
'Meteor'
'Mini Skirt'
'Mystic Charm'
'Pro Legato'
'Purple Passion'
'Ruby Rose'
'Sweet Amber'
'Sundown'
'The Path'
'Yellow Fire'

## Long-lasting blooms
*These last longer than the 1-2 days of average blooms*
'Amber Suzanne'
'Beach Ball'
'Berried Treasure'
'Black Magic'
'Mini Skirt'
'Miss Liberty'

## Suitable as standards
'Fantasia Pink'
'Fantasia White'
'Pink Psyche'
'Sprinkle Rain'

## Suitable as espalier
'General Corteges'
'Rose Scott'
'Ross Estey'
'White Kalakaua' (syn 'Pearl Harbor')

## Attractive foliage
'Columbus' (glossy)
'General Corteges' (dark, sometimes variegated)
'Gold' (glossy)
'Mount Shasta' (very glossy)
'Snow Queen' (striking white variegated)

## Unusual colors
*Flower colors are most distinctive when first open, sometimes later changing. See the main list of tropical hybrids for color descriptions*
'Black Knight'
'Blueberry Tart'
'Corona'
'Creole Flame'
'Dusky Beau'
'Estrella Red'
'Fifth Dimension'
'For Pete's Sake'
'442 Battalion'
'Granny's Bonnet'
'Isobel Beard'
'Lady Cilento'
'Pacific Pearl'
'Purple Passion'
'Wilmae'

# Appendix 3 Hibiscus Facts

1. In Asia, the hibiscus is called the 'shoeshine' or the 'shoeblack' plant because the flower (*H. rosa-sinensis*) can be rubbed over leather to blacken and shine it. This is astonishingly effective.

2. The purplish-black juice from crushed red flowers has been used as a dye, as ink, as coloring for liquors, and to stain paper to make it react like litmus paper. It was also popularly used by women for tinting their hair and eyebrows.

3. In traditional Pacific cultures, the wearing of a hibiscus bloom over the right ear was understood to indicate that the wearer was single and seeking a lover; when worn over the left ear, that the wearer was mated.

4. For floral arrangements, flowers picked from the bush last exactly the same length of time whether or not they are put in water.

5. Hibiscus bark has been used for centuries as a strong fiber for weaving and making cords and ropes. Try taking thin strips off a long hibiscus stem to plait into a rope – it can prove to be extremely strong.

6. Hibiscus are unaffected by the herbicide glyphosate.

7. The species *H. sabdariffa* was once grown as a commercial crop in Australia for producing jam. The fleshy calyxes exude an acidic juice, somewhat like cranberry in flavor, which Jamaicans ferment into a drink. The jam recipe: harvest the calyxes (i.e. what is left after the flower has wilted, containing the seeds) with short stalks attached, and cover them with water. Boil for about 45 to 50 minutes. Strain and cool, then add one cup of sugar for every cup of liquid. Boil until it thickens to a jelly. Cool and bottle.

# Appendix 4: Sources

The importation of live plants and plant materials across borders requires special arrangements, which will be detailed in suppliers' catalogs. Canadians importing plant material must pay a fee and complete an "application for permit to import". Contact:

Plant Health and Production Division
2nd Floor West, Permit Office
59 Camelot Drive
Nepean, Ontario K1A 0Y9.
Fax: (613) 228-6605
Web: www.cfia-acia.agr.ca

**American Hibiscus Society**
PO Box 12073W
St. Petersburg, Florida 33733-2073
Web: www.americanhibiscus.org
*Non-profit society. Annual membership US$17.50 includes publication* The Seed Pod. *Operates hibiscus seed bank. Write to:*
AIIS Seed Bank
171 Green Cove Road
Venice, Florida 34292-2408.

**Exotic Hibiscus**
66282 Cambridge Rd.
Pinellas Park, Florida 33782
Tel: (941) 722-7937
Fax: (941) 721-7896
Web: www.exotichibiscus.com
*Cultivars from hybridizer and exhibitor Curt Sinclair.*

**Hibiscus Hut**
3812 Sandalwood Court
Fairfax, Virginia 22031
Tel: (703) 978-4649
Web: www.hibiscus-hut.com
*Many selections of hardy perennial and annual hibiscus plants and seeds.*

**Hidden Valley Hibiscus**
PMB 281, 2411 East Valley Parkway
Escondido, CA 92027
Tel: (760) 749-6410
Fax: (760) 749-8165
Web: www.exotic-hibiscus.com
*Grafted* Hibiscus rosa-sinensis *hybrids.*

**Logee's Greenhouses, Ltd.**
141 North Street
Danielson, Connecticut 06239-1939
Toll-free Tel: 1-888-330-8038
Toll-free Fax: 1-888-774-9932
Tel: (860) 774-8038
Web: www.logees.com
*Tropical plants since 1872.*

**Stokes Tropicals**
PO Box 9868
New Iberia, Louisiana 70562
Toll-free Tel: 1-800-624-9706
Tel: (337) 365-6998; 365-6991
Fax (337) 365-6991
Web: www.stokestropicals.com
*Large selection of tropical plants.*

**Sunshine Farms**
PO Box 289
Mt. View, Hawaii 96771
Toll-free Tel: 1-800-332-2555
Tel: (808) 968-6312
Fax: (808) 968-8011
*Large variety of tropicals, including hibiscus.*

**Winn Soldani's Fancy Hibiscus**
1142 SW First Avenue
Pompano Beach, Florida 33060-8706
Toll-free Tel: 1-800-432-8332
Tel: (954) 782-0741
Fax: (954) 782-7639
Web: www.fancyhibiscus.com
*250 varieties of tropical fancy hibiscus. Catalog $2.50. Contact regarding shipping to Canada.*

# Index